# TANNENBERG 1914

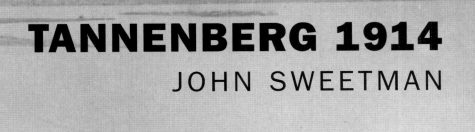

# TANNENBERG 1914

## JOHN SWEETMAN

CASSELL&CO

Cassell & Co
The Orion Publishing Group
Wellington House
125 Strand
London WC2R 0BB

A catalogue record for this book is available
from the British Library

ISBN 0-304-35635-2

Designed by Goldust Design
Printed and bound in Spain

# CONTENTS

# LIST OF MAPS

# FOREWORD

In the first volume of his important book *The First World War* Hew Strachan emphasises that 'the war was global from the outset,' and goes on to devote much of his attention to events outside Western Europe. As far as Russia is concerned such diversification is long overdue, for, despite Norman Stone's groundbreaking *The Eastern Front 1914-1917*, the fighting in the east has received far less attention than that in the west. This reflects the marked tendency for the history of the war to be written along national lines and for events on the Western Front to dominate its historiography in English.

Yet even historians who, like me, have concentrated on the Western Front, cannot deny the importance of the Eastern Front in what was, from start to finish, a coalition war. There are many examples. As we shall see, in 1914 Tannenberg had an indirect effect on the campaign in France, and in March 1916 the Russians launched a costly attack at Lake Narotch in an effort to take the pressure off the French at Verdun. They followed it with the Brussilov offensive which did indeed persuade the Germans to swing troops eastwards and induced Romania (unwisely, in the event) to enter the war.

In 1914 German and Austrian planners had to acknowledge that Russian military capacity was steadily improving, even if its operational application was uncertain and its increase was from a start-point well behind that of other major armies. In pre-war talks the French pressed the Russians to take the offensive by the fifteenth day of mobilization, and in 1913 it was specified that one-third of a loan raised in Paris for Russian railways should be applied to military railways. Hew Strachan adds, however, that Russia agreed to take a rapid offensive against Germany 'as much to suit its own needs as to assuage French anxieties.' The Russians were (rightly) concerned about war in the Balkans, recognised (again rightly) that Austria–Hungary would be unlikely to act against them without the promise of German support, and (perhaps most rightly of all) had begun to see that Germany would first turn against France and then swing eastwards to deal with Russia at their leisure. Thus both the logic of the French alliance and the demands of national strategy suggested an immediate offensive.

However, as John Sweetman shows so well, although the Russian Army was strong in raw manpower – with almost 1.5 million men under arms before the war, a total which would be doubled on mobilization, it was Europe's largest – that manpower was, despite the efforts of the reformers, still patchily trained and equipped. And it was an ethnic melting-pot, drawn from an empire stretching from the Arctic to Afghanistan. But perhaps most serious, it was an army corroded by factionalism, whose transport, communications and staff procedures were to prove sadly unequal to the Germans. The Russian offensive plan was strategically logical and tactically feasible: but it was a plan which asked too much of the system tasked with executing it. Yet, as this book demonstrates, there was nothing wrong with Russian courage, with these soldiers 'with honest Russian faces,' too many of whom were 'only peasants in disguise.' In an early successful attack one regiment lost nine of its sixteen company commanders, and a single company had 120 of 190 men killed.

Early Russian successes sent their ripples wide. Moltke, the German commander-in-chief, reacted to news of the Russian advance by sending two corps and a cavalry division from the western front to the east. His chief of operations was to maintain that this was a mistake, which contributed to German defeat on the Marne, while the future Marshal Foch, then a newly-appointed army commander, was later to declare that this diversion significantly eased the Allied task in that battle. John Sweetman is less convinced, suggesting that the Germans made serious command errors on the Marne and the absent divisions could not have tilted the balance. However, their departure unquestionably contributed to the steady erosion of German forces in the west, to which battle casualties and losses on a long line of march also contributed. Tannenberg did indeed make a difference, albeit an indirect one. And in propaganda terms – the naming of the battle was deeply symbolic – Tannenberg went some way towards counterbalancing the absence of a victory in the west, where it really mattered.

Tannenberg had a more direct effect on the Russian Army. It did lasting damage to its self-confidence, but failed to initiate that thoroughgoing reform of its high command which was so urgently required. It deprived Russia of both equipment and trained officers which she could ill afford to lose. And, lastly, it played its own baneful part in the process which was to persuade so many of the wearers of those honest Russian faces that the spell of tsarism was broken forever.

RICHARD HOLMES

# PREFACE

Reflecting on the Battle of Tannenberg twenty-five years later, Captain B.H. Liddell Hart wrote: 'No battle has caused more controversy, [or] produced so large a literature in so short a time'.[1] During the decade after the German Eighth Army clashed with the Russian First, Second and, belatedly, Tenth armies in East Prussia during the autumn of 1914, many of the surviving protagonists polished their ego in print and eagerly besmirched the reputation of others, not all from the opposite side. Furthermore, a wide range of international authors have subsequently picked over the bones of a campaign, whose far-reaching military and political implications were masked in August 1914 by western preoccupation with German columns marching through Belgium to invade France.

A pot-pourri of contrary opinions and explanations has been advanced over the years. German success removed a direct military threat to Berlin; on the other hand, the tsar's troops frustrated an attack on their own homeland. From the Russian standpoint, the entire exercise represented a costly, irrelevant sideshow, which diverted valuable forces away from the main enemy, Austria–Hungary; apologists respond by insisting that military obligations had to be met in the cause of political integrity. For, in pre-war staff talks, the Russian Army had been committed to aggressive action against Germany fifteen days after mobilization to relieve pressure on the nation's ally, France. Tactically, critics hold that the Russian commanders were incompetent; supporters maintain they were hamstrung by a naive strategic plan and the trappings of an inept administrative system. In terms of personalities, dispute continues to ferment over whether Erich Ludendorff, Paul von Hindenburg (his superior), or Max Hoffmann (a more junior staff officer) was the architect of German victory. However, the swift removal from post of the North-West Front commander, General Y.G. Zhilinski, suggests that he was primarily responsible for the Russian defeat; or perhaps he presented a convenient scapegoat.

The German choice of Tannenberg as the name of the battle highlighted 500 years of festering bitterness at a humiliation suffered in 1410. The 'Tannenberg' confrontation of 1914, though, was not a single encounter decided in one day but a campaign which spread throughout much of East Prussia from 17 August until 13 September; a period effectively extended by skirmishes in the weeks immediately before and after. Of the three and a half armies involved, two suffered 50 per cent loss in casualties and prisoners. Beyond that bald statistic, and in the light of the conflicting conclusions about the reasons for it, there is much still to ponder and debate.

Eastern Europe c.1410

SWEDEN

Stockholm

Gotland

Öland

*Baltic Sea*

Pomerania

Danzig

Königsberg

Marienburg

TEUTONIC ORDER

Prussia

Courland

Reval

Estonia

Livonia

Riga

Samogitia

Dünaburg

Gulf of Finland

Lake
Ladoga

to
Moscovy

Novgorod

Novgorod

Pskov

Pskov

Polotsk

Vitebsk

Smolensk

Smolensk

Tver

Tver

Moscovy

Moscow

Tula

RY

Rosto

Kovno

Vilna

Niemen

Novgorod

Minsk

Polotsk

Chernigov

LITHUANIA

Mazovia

Poznan

Warsaw

Czersk

POLAND

Vistula

Pinsk

Pinsk

Pripet
Marshes

Chernigov

Chernigov

Kiev

Kiev

Pereyaslav

Don

Dniepr

Breslau

Silesia

Sandomierz

Volyn

Kracow

Lvov

Moravia

Podolia

Halicz

Kassa

Slovakia

Debrecen

Dniester

Suceava

Bug

COSSACKS

CRIMEAN TARTA

Buda

HUNGARY

Pruth

MOLDAVIA

Khadzhi-Bei

Castrum Illicis
(Oleshe)

Sea of A

Crimea

Transylvania

to Genoa

Moncastro
(Akkerman)

to Genoa

Kaffa

to Ger

Gazarie

Belgrade

BOSNIA

SERBIA

WALLACHIA

N

*Black Sea*

BULGARIA

0          200 km

0                    20

# PROLOGUE: HISTORICAL LEGACY

As dawn broke on the morning of Wednesday 15 July 1410, two medieval armies prepared for battle on a small, undulating plain speckled with occasional trees and sparse copses near the village of Tannenberg, 90 miles south-east of the Baltic port of Gdansk (Danzig). That of the Order of Teutonic Knights under their Grand Master Ulrich von Jungingen faced a force led by Jagiello (Vladislav II), ruler of Poland and Lithuania, which had invaded Pruthenia (Prussia) intent on capturing Marienburg, its capital. Before the day closed, one commander would perish with a great many of his men; his conqueror record a momentous victory.

**Eastern Europe c.1410**

The Knights deployed an assembly of well-disciplined armoured horsemen, supplemented by English archers and Genoese crossbowmen. They possessed several artillery pieces including a massive 9 tonne cannon firing stone shot weighing 450 kilograms; indeed, both armies were credited with rudimentary artillery, though none of it played a significant part in the action. Theoretically the Knights were a coherent, experienced body, their opponents infinitely less so. The Poles, lacking both experience and cohesion, could field fewer armoured knights and the majority of their infantry were ill-equipped peasants carrying a motley collection of flails, spears and farm implements such as forks and scythes. The Lithuanian contingent under Jagiello's cousin, Grand Duke Vitold, included Ruthenians and Tartars from subordinate provinces and its knights rode smaller horses than the Poles. Many of them

**Jagiello (c.1351–1434).** In 1386 Grand Duke Jagiello of Lithuania married the Polish queen Jadwiga (c.1373–1399) and was crowned Vladislav II of Poland. Following Jadwiga's death, he remained king of Poland with Lithuania governed by his cousin Grand Duke Vitold.

were protected with leather not mail. Some infantry levies wore leather coats and helmets, but like their Polish counterparts all were poorly armed, many simply with lassos. Nevertheless, together the combined force would be 'of imposing size and unusual diversity'; knights, 'turbulent Russian boyars or the rude skin-clad Samogitians', 'thousands of Tartars … martial Lithuanians'. Jungingen bitingly dismissed the Lithuanians as 'more at home with a spoon than with a sword'; a fatal miscalculation.[1]

Singing the traditional hymn of St Adalbert, on 9 July the invaders crossed the Polish frontier to close on Kurzetnik, 25 miles north-west, en route for Marienburg. Although Jagiello retained overall command of his two armies, Zyndram of Maszkowice led the Poles in the field. Short of Kurzetnik on the opposite bank of the Drweca river, Jagiello's armies camped around Lake Rubkowo. Armed scouts returned with the unpalatable news that the Knights were strongly entrenched across the river. A frontal attack would be suicidal, so Jagiello opted for evasion.

His armies, therefore, struck camp on Monday 13 July to march eastwards with the intention of skirting the village of Grünwald and approaching Marienburg from the flank. They soon overcame strong resistance from the garrison of Dabrowno. Meanwhile, learning that the Polish camp was empty, Jungingen assumed that Jagiello had retreated across the frontier once more and set off southwards. With the fall of Dabrowno, the Grand Master realized that he had been outwitted. Detaching 3,000 men under Heinrich von Plauen to Marienburg, he took the rest of his force towards Grünwald and Tannenberg, aiming to bring the Polish king to battle on the 2-mile square plain just south of the villages. He had no qualms about achieving an overwhelming victory. The ultimate casualties suggest that an estimate of over 100,000 Poles and Lithuanians engaging 83,000 with the Teutonic Order may not be exaggerated.

Battle
of Tannenberg
15 July 1410

Below: Phase 1
Next page:
Phases 2 and 3

During the night of 14–15 July 1410 thunder, lightning and high winds hampered the two armies, which seemingly remained unclear about the strength and precise position of each other. At sunrise, however, it became evident that the Knights had made extraordinary progress north-eastwards from their attempt to intercept Jagiello's phantom flight from the Drweca river. They were now drawn up in battle order, confident that they would prevent any further advance on Marienburg. The bulk of Jagiello's army had camped in woods close to Lake Lubien about 4.5 miles east of Grünwald and 3 miles north of Dabrowno. The initiative lay with the Knights. Jagiello must get past them to reach Marienburg. On the other hand, Jungingen could not afford to attack Jagiello in the woods and must provoke him into fighting on ground of Teutonic choosing.

KEY

| | |
|---|---|
| | Teutonic Horse |
| | Teutonic Infantry |
| | Teutonic Artillery |
| ✕ | Teutonic Obstacles |
| ⚑ | Grand Master's Command Post |
| ✕ | Skirmishers |
| | Polish Forces |
| | Lithuanian-Ruthenian Forces |

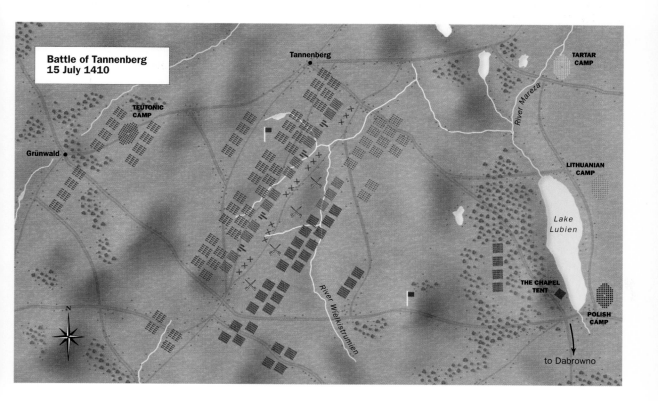

**Battle of Tannenberg
15 July 1410**

Tannenberg

TARTAR CAMP

TEUTONIC CAMP

River Mareza

Grünwald

LITHUANIAN CAMP

Lake Lubien

THE CHAPEL TENT

River Wielkistrumien

POLISH CAMP

N

to Dabrowno

Phase 2

N

0                    500 yards

Tannenberg

Grünwald

TEUTONIC
CAMP

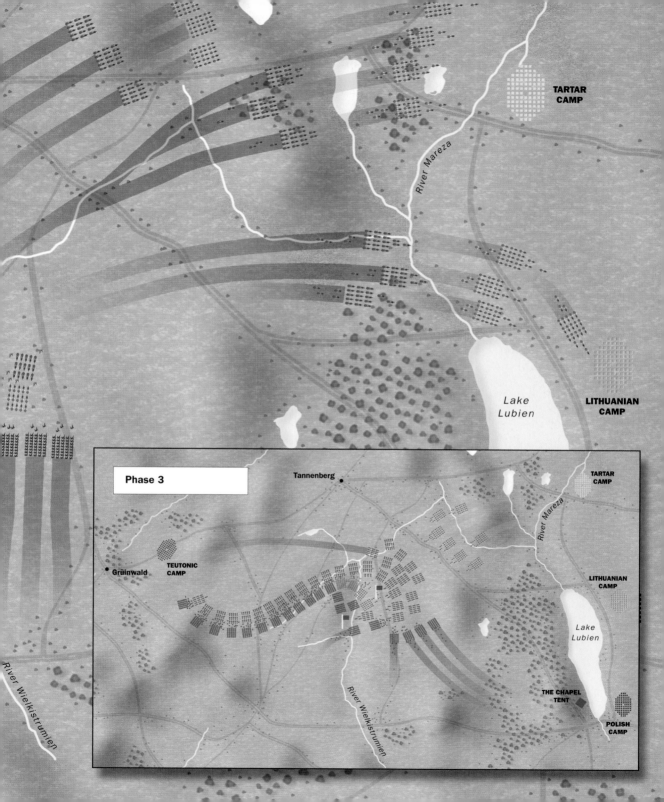

TARTAR
CAMP

River Mareza

Lake
Lubien

LITHUANIAN
CAMP

**Phase 3**

Tannenberg

TARTAR
CAMP

Grünwald

TEUTONIC
CAMP

LITHUANIAN
CAMP

Lake
Lubien

River Wielkistrumien

THE CHAPEL
TENT

River Mareza

POLISH
CAMP

River Wielkistrumien

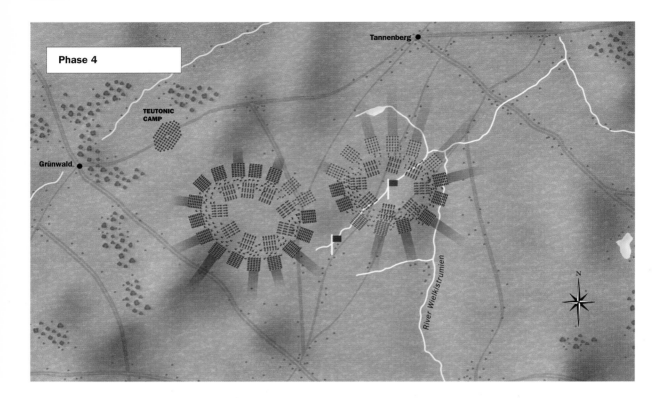

Phase 4

TEUTONIC CAMP

Tannenberg

Grünwald

River Wielki Strumien

N

**KEY**

Teutonic Horse

Teutonic Infantry

Teutonic Artillery

Teutonic Obstacles

Grand Master's Command Post

Skirmishers

Polish Forces

Lithuanian-Ruthenian Forces

**Battle of Tannenberg 15 July 1410 Phase 4**

The Polish king showed no sign of urgency, spending hours in prayer – possibly a delaying tactic while the rest of his troops came up from Dabrowno. Meanwhile the impatient Vitold mustered his Lithuanians north-west of the lake, while Zyndram deployed the Poles west and south of it. By 9 a.m., Polish skirmishers had identified the main Teuton position, protected by ditches and other obstacles. Infantry and cannon formed the Knights' front line, with cavalry in support to exploit and pursue a disorganized attacker. In mid-morning, from rising ground in advance of their two armies, the respective commanders surveyed the ground. By now an early breeze had died away, and the temperature soared on a bright, sunny day.

Stalemate prevailed until midday. Jungingen then sent two knights to parley, each provocatively carrying a sword with no sheath. They told Jagiello that 'Grand Master Ulrich sends you through us, his heralds, these two swords to help you in the coming strife', which might be an encouragement to act 'with greater courage'. Declaring that 'this astonishing arrogance of our enemies the Lord of Battles and just Judge will vanquish and humiliate', Jagiello gave the order to advance.[2]

The Polish formations moved forward steadily on the left, but on the right Vitold's eager horsemen charged wildly ahead, their impetus carrying them through the infantry vanguard and interspersed cannon until halted and driven back in disarray by Jungingen's cavalry reserve. Many scattered to the east, and Vitold hurried to Jagiello at his command post in the rear urging him to show himself on the field. The Knights were threatening to swing round behind the Poles, blocked only by three Russian squadrons from Smolensk, which stood firm under immense pressure. Jagiello's appearance encouraged many of the Lithuanians to return to the fray and steadied wavering mercenaries on the Polish left. For there, following two salvos from their guns, Teutonic horsemen had debouched from behind a ridge south of Grünwald. A furious fight ensued on the Polish left amid clouds of dust, during which several banners were lost or fell on the ground. Following a sudden shower of rain and the arrival of reinforcements, the Poles gradually gained the initiative.

**Next page:**

**Battle of Tannenberg, 15 July 1410.**
In July 1410, Polish and Lithuanian forces advanced into Pruthenia (Prussia) towards Marienburg, the Teutonic Knights' capital. They lured the Knights from their strong defensive position and routed them on a small plain south of Grünwald (the Polish name for the encounter) and Tannenberg.

On the allied right the tide of battle had also begun to swing in favour of the attackers. Seeing the confusion of the Lithuanians, Jungingen led sixteen fresh cavalry squadrons forward. One made for Jagiello's entourage, where the royal banner was unfurled. The situation was grave. A Polish squadron asked to support its monarch replied that 'if we turn our backs on the enemy, we shall be in still greater peril'.[3] As the Teutonic squadrons advanced, one knight broke ranks to gallop at Jagiello. The king was saved by Zbigniew of Olensia, who unseated then killed the would-be assassin. The sixteen Teutonic

squadrons had fatally halted, while this critical episode was played out. Their hesitation allowed the revitalized Lithuanians to surround and annihilate them – one more costly Teutonic error. The Grand Master and several of his leading officials perished. By 6 p.m. the Knights were in full retreat, having suffered an estimated 32,000 casualties including prisoners, plus the indignity of losing all their fifty-one standards; underscoring 'one of the most splendid victories in Polish history … [of] unequalled moral significance'.[4]

Tannenberg was a critical encounter. The Poles celebrated it as the glorious Battle of Grünwald; the Germans never forgot the defeat, which stemmed their eastward progress and effectively destroyed the power and prestige of the Teutonic Knights. They would wait half a millennium for an opportunity to obliterate the humiliation of that fateful day. This time, Russian troops would invade the German homeland from Poland; the battlefield extend for 100, not 2 miles; the conflict last far beyond a single day.

As he prepared for battle in East Prussia in August 1914, General Paul Ludwig Hans Anton von Beneckendorff und von Hindenburg mused that 'there were many who bore my name among the Teutonic Knights, who went out … to fight heathendom and Poland' at the first Battle of Tannenberg.[5] For him that distant page of national history remained sharply in focus.

## POLITICAL BACKGROUND

**A**fter defeating France in the Franco-Prussian War (1870–71) and seeing the German Empire proclaimed in the Palace of Versailles, Prince Otto von Bismarck, the German Chancellor, quickly recognized the need to avoid a war on two fronts; the nightmare scenario of Germany crushed between the nutcracker of a resentful France in co-operation with Russia or Austria–Hungary. Noting that 'our principal concern is to keep the peace between our two imperial neighbours' (Russia and Austria–Hungary), Bismarck disingenuously referred to 'the aggressive, plundering instincts' of France.[1] Thus, after careful diplomacy, in 1873 he engineered the signing of the *Dreikaiserbund*, whereby Germany, Russia and Austria–Hungary would confer if any of them were threatened by another European power, and would send troops in support should war break out. Austria–Hungary and Russia,

however, had conflicting interests in the Balkans. So six years later, the more binding Dual Alliance was signed between Germany and Austria–Hungary, whereby each would come to the other's aid if attacked by Russia and remain neutral if attacked by another European power (by implication, France). Should Russia combine with that other power, both were pledged to fight. Thus Bismarck had apparently ensured active support should a war on two fronts (involving Russia and France) develop.

In 1882 Italy joined the central powers to form the Triple Alliance, with a secret addendum excusing her from fighting Britain. Although the *Dreikaiserbund* theoretically remained operative, it lapsed in 1887 when Austria–Hungary refused renewal; a German–Russian bilateral substitute proved short-lived. Once Bismarck had left office in 1890, the German connection with Russia was firmly broken and the tsar looked elsewhere for reassurance. When he turned to France the spectre of a war on two fronts revived.

**Prince Otto Eduard Leopold Bismarck (1815–1898),** Chief Minister of Prussia (1862–1890), and Chancellor of the new German Empire (1871–1890).

**Opposite: General Yakov Grigorevich Zhilinski (1853–1918),** centre, presenting awards to Russian officers.

## MILITARY UNDERTAKINGS

An entente promising consultation between France and Russia was signed in 1891. In August 1892 this was expanded into a military convention guaranteeing positive commitment of forces should either become embroiled in war with Germany, which was ratified by both countries in December 1893. With the aim of co-ordinating action to prevent the Triple Alliance concentrating on one of them and at the same time obliging it to disperse its forces, members of the respective military staffs conferred between 1893 and 1913. The outcome of these conferences was to prove crucial, ultimately decisive when war eventually broke out. Arguing that defeat of the dominant partner, Germany, would fatally undermine Austria–Hungary's resolve to fight on, the French pressed Russia to take the field fifteen days after the commencement of her mobilization ('M+15'). Given the vast area over which concentration

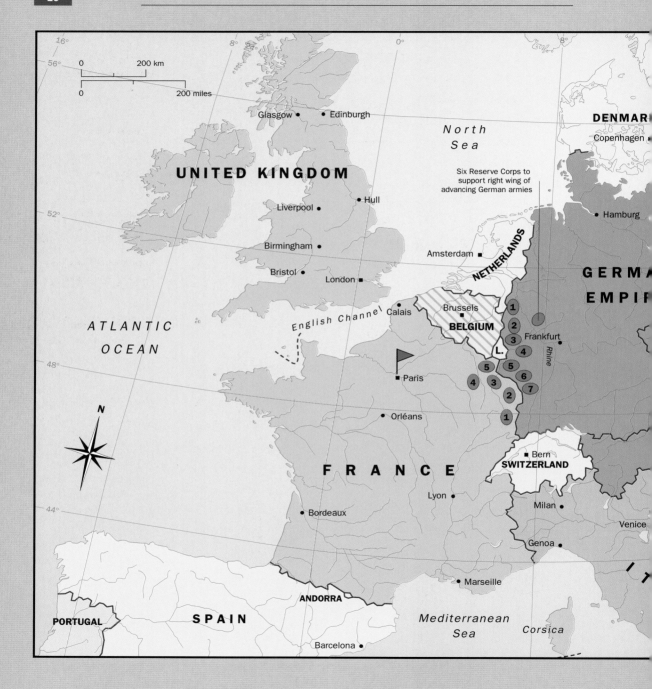

Six Reserve Corps to
support right wing of
advancing German armies

**Europe in 1914:**
**two armed camps**

Austro-German Alliance,
1879–1918

Triple Alliance, 1882–1915

Franco-Russian Alliance,
1893–1917

Triple Entente, 1907–1917

varying independence and
nationalist movements sponsored
by Russia, 1879–1914

sympathetic to 'Central Powers'

sympathetic to 'Entente Powers'

neutrality guaranteed by United
Kingdom

neutral

⑤ approximate planned army
positions in July, 1914

of her forces must be achieved and the rudimentary nature of Russia's transport system, this would entail a massive undertaking. Yet in August 1911 at Krasnoe Selo General Y.G. Zhilinski, Chief of the General Staff (CGS), provisionally agreed and a year later in Paris committed the Russian Army to a major campaign 'after M+15', when only one third of its men had been mobilized. The French representative at the 1912 Paris conference (General J.J.C. Joffre) also secured specific agreement to strike north-west from the Narew river over the frontier towards Allenstein, if the Germans concentrated in East Prussia. As Russia would inevitably fight aggressively against Austria–Hungary in Galicia, this meant offensives on both northern and southern fronts. Zhilinski went even further in August 1913, more precisely undertaking to have 800,000 men ready to face Germany 'in the main by the 15th day of mobilization'. In the opinion of a tsarist officer, Lieutenant General N.N. Golovine, together these different commitments constituted 'a strategic error of the first magnitude'.[2]

The probability of the so-called Dual Entente between France and Russia being widened grew in 1904, when Britain came to an agreement with France over the countries' respective colonial interests. In December 1905 secret staff talks began between Britain and France, which centred on co-operation in time of war. By 1911 this evolved into a military commitment (without overt political endorsement) for 150,000 British infantry and cavalry to land in France by the twelfth day of mobilization. The Director-General of Military Operations at the War Office in London (Major General H.H. Wilson) warned that in the event of conflict between Germany and France, France might be defeated before Russia could mobilize in fulfilment of her treaty obligations. In 1912 a naval understanding allocated the Mediterranean to France, the North Sea to Britain. Morally, if not legally, Britain had joined the anti-German camp. She had been politically even further committed in 1907, when a colonial agreement on spheres of influence, notably in Persia, was concluded with Russia. However loosely, a Triple Entente now peered menacingly across German frontiers in the west and east (Germany and Russia having shared a common border since Poland ceased to exist as an independent state in 1795).

## THE SCHLIEFFEN PLAN

As Bismarck demonstrated, the prospect of war on two fronts had long been feared. In 1860 the Chief of the General Staff, General Count Helmuth von Moltke, mused about the danger of 'co-operation between the Slav East and the Latin West against the centre of Europe'.[3] Eleven years later he argued that in the wake of her defeat by Germany, France would prove the lesser threat. In 1879 he outlined a defensive plan to cope with France, while German troops attacked Russia from east of the Vistula towards the Narew river, with the Austrians simultaneously advancing further south through Galicia. France would be tackled once Russia succumbed. Moltke's immediate successor General Count Alfred von Waldersee concurred. So initially did General Count Alfred von Schlieffen, who became Chief of the General Staff in 1891. Within four years Schlieffen began to revise his opinion.

Serious social unrest, involving a rash of strikes and violent disturbances deploring social injustice which intensified in the early years of the twentieth century, committed the Russian Army to extensive internal security operations. Then it became embroiled in the Russo-Japanese War (1904–5), which starkly exposed Russian military weakness to the world. Following completion of the Trans-Siberian railway in 1901, Russia sought to expand her territory and influence in the Far East. This brought conflict with Japan, which especially coveted Port Arthur (leased by Russia from China), Korea and Manchuria. Serious naval reverses for Russia were supplemented by a carillon of defeats ashore on the banks of the Yalu river, at Liaoyang north of Port Arthur, on the Shaho river and, decisively, at Mukden.

In the subsequent Treaty of Portsmouth, Russia surrendered Port Arthur, evacuated Manchuria and recognized Korea as a Japanese sphere of influence.

**Field Marshal Count Alfred von Schlieffen (c.1833–1913).** As Chief of the German General Staff, Schlieffen prepared for a war on two fronts. His celebrated Plan envisaged defeating France in six weeks, then turning on Russia.

Specifically, the Russian troops under 57-year-old General Alexei Kuropatkin displayed tactical naivety, misunderstood the importance of barbed wire and machine guns and were short of effective artillery. They had been routed by an enemy force of equal strength, which advanced overland from Korea and ejected the Russians from defensive positions which they had ample time to prepare. Max Hoffmann (a German military observer with the Japanese) high-lighted command shortcomings in claiming that 'in every battle Kuropatkin ... had victory in his hand, he only required to have the firm resolution of closing his hand in order to grasp the victory', but supinely failed to do so.[4] Overall, the Russians incurred 385,000 casualties; the Japanese 167,000.

**Field Marshal Count Helmuth Karl Bernhard von Moltke (1800–1891), 'the Elder'.**

To Germany the Russians now appeared much less of a threat than the French. The huge levy exacted in 1871, which Bismarck had hoped would emasculate France for ten years, had been paid off in little over two. Twenty years later France could finance massive loans to her new ally, Russia. Rapid expansion of roads, canals and railways provided a transport infrastructure, which helped to produce a six-fold rise in the output of iron and coal in the generation after 1870. Short-service engagements and reorganization of the reserves created a potential army of 2 million men, and fortresses along France's eastern frontier were strengthened.

Based on these developments, between December 1905 and January 1906, Schlieffen produced the plan, which bears his name and had evolved through several drafts over ten years. In 1897 he wrote that to outflank the French fron-tier fortresses Germany 'must not shrink from violating the neutrality of Belgium as well as Luxembourg'. Eight years later he declared that, to avoid the strongholds of Namur and Liège, his armies should also march through southern Holland to execute successfully 'the great wheel'.[5] To produce the preponderance of men required for this exercise, Schlieffen pared forces allo-cated to the eastern front. In the west he envisaged the deployment of seven German armies, their strength enhanced by trained reservists, along the French frontier from Switzerland to Liège, with just one army guarding East

**Battle of Tsu-shima, 27 May 1905.** During the Russo-Japanese War (1904–5), a Russian fleet sailed from St Petersburg via the Atlantic and Indian oceans to relieve Port Arthur in Manchuria. It was annihilated in the Tsu-shima Straits off south Korea.

Prussia against the Russians. The celebrated Schlieffen Plan foresaw three of the western armies sucking the French into Alsace and Lorraine (lost to Germany in 1871) by acting defensively. Meanwhile, the four armies north of the Moselle river were scheduled to advance into France, three consolidating east of Paris northwards from the fortress of Verdun, one swinging west of the French capital. The critical blow administered by this right wing of the German line-up through the Low Countries would defeat France in six weeks.

**The Schlieffen Plans 1905 and 1914**

Original Schlieffen Plan, 1905

Execution of modified Schlieffen Plan, August 1914

German army concentration

Schlieffen calculated that Russia would take three months to mobilize and therefore allocated only 5 per cent of his army (some 50,000 men) to defend East Prussia, which he accepted might be invaded sooner than expected. Should that happen, he conceived a defensive campaign involving possible withdrawal to the Vistula river gaining time for reinforcements to arrive once France had been overcome. In his last memorandum, dated 28 December 1912, Schlieffen commented specifically on Russia's poor rail network and need to distribute regiments throughout her large empire to deal with domestic unrest. According to his son-in-law, Major Wilhelm von Hanke, just before he died in 1913 Schlieffen murmured: 'It must come to a fight. Only make the right wing strong'.[6]

After Schlieffen left office in 1906, his successor General Helmuth von Moltke, the elder Moltke's nephew, undermined chances of rapid success in the west by excluding Holland (the Netherlands) from the equation to provide an international trade conduit for Germany with neutral countries. Moltke also doubted the ability of German forces to achieve the speed of advance anticipated by Schlieffen. Instead of simply holding in the south, he looked towards double envelopment of the French field armies. Moltke thus strengthened the German Fifth, Sixth and Seventh armies to the detriment of the northern thrust and ordered these formations to be ready to drive forward to meet the German First Army's sweep around Paris. To do so he weakened Schlieffen's intended northern (right) wing by seventeen divisions. Under

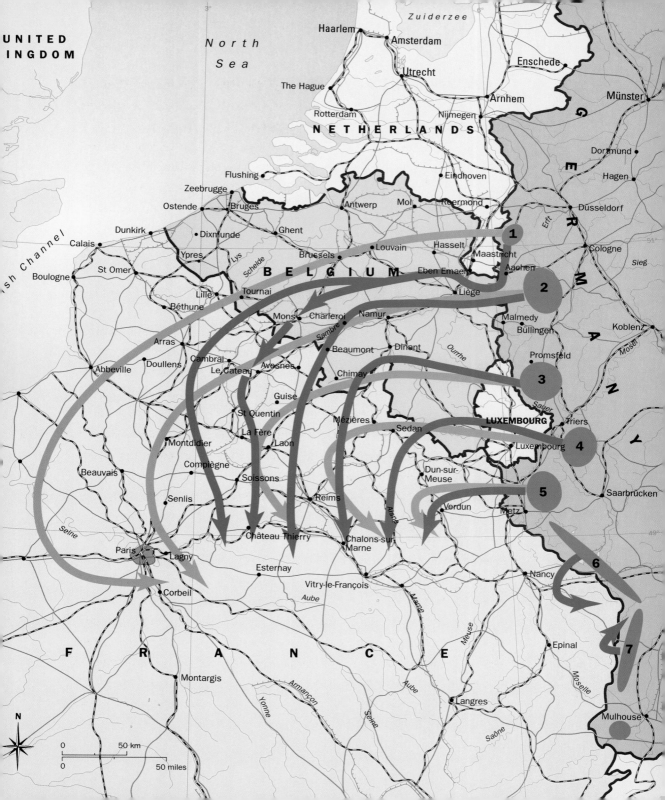

**Sarajevo, 28 June 1914.**
During a visit to Bosnia, following a failed assassination attempt earlier that day, Archduke Franz Ferdinand and his wife leave the Town Hall. Shortly afterwards, they were shot dead in their open car, and the countdown to the First World War commenced.

pressure from influential East Prussian landowners, he further depleted the overall western force by increasing the troops in East Prussia to 15 per cent of available strength. A 200,000 strong Eighth Army, deployed behind the 60 mile long barrier of the Masurian Lakes and stiffened by fortifications in its vicinity, should be capable of resisting a Russian invasion before the fall of France. Having read Moltke's revised version of Schlieffen's plan in May 1914, a German general reputedly declared: 'Good, now we are ready. The sooner it starts, the better for us!'[7]

## IMPENDING CRISIS

Between 20 and 24 April 1914 a significant series of Russian war games took place in the Kiev Military District based on the proposition that Russia and France were at war with the Triple Alliance; Russia had mobilized and awaited

active involvement in the conflict. In this exercise, the main Russian force deployed against Austria–Hungary with the North-West Front covering its flank and fulfilling political obligations by attracting to it 'the largest possible number of the German forces, with the object of denuding the French front of German troops'.[8] On the ninth day of mobilization, Zhilinski (acting as the North-West Front commander) was told that German formations had invaded Russian territory west of the Niemen river. He decided to attack three days later, sending his First Army against the flank and rear of the invaders, with the Second Army engaging them from the south on the fourteenth day of mobilization. Golovine later castigated this 'light-hearted decision to assume the offensive', given the inevitable state of the two armies' unreadiness so soon after the commencement of mobilisation. He contended that Zhilinski displayed 'a complete misunderstanding of the conditions of a modern battle'

**Arrest of Gavrilo Princip (1894–1918).**
The 19-year-old Bosnian Serb student plotted the assassination of Archduke Franz Ferdinand in Belgrade, and Austria–Hungary held Servia responsible for his crime. Princip was quickly seized, and sentenced to 20 years hard labour.

and vastly underestimated the capability of opposing German units.[9] However, the summary issued by the Ministry of War on 22 May merely described rather than analysed, still less criticized, the decisions taken and movements ordered by participants. Zhilinski, therefore, psychologically departed with tacit approval for a two-pronged offensive of his First Army followed by the Second Army within a fortnight of mobilization.

On 28 June 1914 a 19-year-old Bosnian Serb, Gavrilo Princip, assassinated the Archduke Franz Ferdinand, heir to the Austro-Hungarian throne, and his wife in Sarajevo. Europe rapidly slipped over the abyss. The fatal act proved a catalyst for war, a time to settle old scores. In 1908 Austria–Hungary had annexed the Slav territories of Bosnia and Herzegovina. Still recovering from the Russo-Japanese War and riven with domestic unrest, Russia merely protested. She could not afford to stand aside again. Perceptively, Bismarck forecast that 'some damned foolish thing in the Balkans' would ignite a major European conflict. It emerged that Princip was a member of a Servian nationalist society, The Black Hand, and had plotted his deed in Belgrade. Assured of German support, on 23 July Austria–Hungary delivered a crushing ultimatum to Servia, which two days later accepted all but one condition. To no avail. Austria–Hungary declared war on 28 July. Having failed to persuade Germany to restrain her ally, the tsar signed mobilization orders on 30 July (effective the following day); 'in Russia the indignation, which I share, is tremendous', wrote Nicholas II. When Russia ignored her demand to stop movements along their common border and cancel mobilization, Germany declared war on 1 August. Two days later she did so on France. Once Germany had violated Belgian neutrality, on 4 August Britain declared war; prompting the German Foreign Minister (Theobald von Bethmann-Hollweg) famously to condemn Britain for the 'unthinkable … just for a word "neutrality" … just for a scrap of paper'; refering to British adherence to the 1839 international treaty guaranteeing Belgian neutrality. Only Italy of the pre-1914 alliance partners stayed out.[10]

## RUSSIAN FORCES

A Russian invasion of East Prussia depended on the speed and effectiveness of general mobilization, which began in earnest on 31 July 1914. The programme aimed at concentrating one third of the field army within fifteen days, a further third in twenty three days and the final third after forty days. However, as the initial muster would comprise the best trained, it was intended that this part of the army would be ready for offensive action by 20 August (twenty-one days after mobilization). The Russians aimed to deploy ten armies along their western frontier in three fronts (army groups): North-West facing Germany; South-West confronting Austria–Hungary; Caucasus against Turkey.

Although he expressed satisfaction with the strength of the cavalry, a senior Russian commander during the First World War, General A.A. Brussilov, had

**Nicholas II
(1868–1918).**
Became tsar in
1894, promoted an
International Peace
Congress at The
Hague (1899), but
vigorously opposed
political and social
reform at home.
Unrest within Russia
led to his abdication
and imprisonment in
1917, his execution
and that of his family
the following year.

serious doubts about the overall effectiveness of the army, which was in the throes of reorganization and development. It would, he judged, not be 'properly prepared for a trial of … strength before 1917'.[1] War in 1914 sharply pre-empted that utopian dream. Despite his aversion to violence and the trappings of military pomp, Brussilov credited Tsar Alexander III with 'most conscientious attention … the most thorough of preparations' of the armed forces. Alexander's son, who succeeded him in 1894, was not so supportive. Nicholas II's personal vacillation, replacement of his father's principal advisers and his reliance on the vain and self-indulgent Kuropatkin as Minister of War quickly undermined Alexander's achievements. By 1909 even sensitive frontier areas like Warsaw District lacked adequate military transport and equipment.

From General Headquarters (GHQ) in Baranovichi, 220 miles north-east of Warsaw, the 58-year-old Commander-in-Chief General of Cavalry Grand Duke Nikolai Nikolaievich supervised all ten Russian armies as well as the entire military organization of the country on the tsar's behalf. He was assisted principally by the 46-year-old Chief of Staff Lieutenant General N.N. Yanushkevich and 48-year-old Major General Yuri Danilov (the Quartermaster General (QMG)), who before the war was closely involved with evolution of the plans to invade East Prussia. As a tangible sign of the advent of aerial warfare, in support of their armies the Russians deployed 244 aeroplanes, whose reconnaissance role would be quite literally vital. A contemporary British statistical survey noted that the Russians had 'numerous skilful and daring aviators, but [were] not very well equipped'. The British military attaché, Brigadier General A.W.F. Knox, thought that the fifteen available airships were militarily useless; the total output of aero-engines by Russian factories was only about twenty-three per month. Brussilov agreed that

Russian airships were 'out-of-date, inefficient, and of no practical value'; the sparse number of aeroplanes similarly 'out-of-date and of little utility'. What is more the air service, as an integral part of the army, was subject to direction by field commanders frequently unsympathetic to its use.[2]

Brussilov was critical of other aspects of the Russian forces as well. The main infantry rifle had proved its worth, but the allocation of just eight machine guns per regiment was, to his mind, totally inadequate: eight per battalion were required, two per company. He calculated that each regiment should have a minimum of forty, making 160 to each division, against the current pitiful thirty-two. The artillery, too, had been woefully neglected. Pre-war practice was intermittent and virtually no attention was paid to firing barrages in support of the infantry. Brussilov argued that batteries of eight guns were 'unquestionably' too large for effective control, six more manageable. Field guns effectively fired shrapnel, but not percussion shells; the lack of heavy artillery represented a major deficiency. A Russian army corps had 108 artillery pieces (ninety-six field and a mere twelve heavy guns) to the German equivalent of 166 pieces, including thirty-six howitzers; and widespread shortage of artillery ammunition constituted 'a sheer catastrophe'.[3]

Lieutenant General N.N. Golovine, who as a colonel commanded a cavalry regiment at the outset of hostilities before progressing to high staff appointments, expressed less pessimism. 'Our front-line troops were up to the necessary standard as regards fighting qualities and tactical organisation', their 'standard of musketry [at] a higher level than in any other army in the world'; the field artillery pieces 'were the superiors not only of the enemy, but even of the French who have always been granted the honour of first place'. Hyperbole; but he was well placed to point to Russia's inferior cavalry, which had not 'rid itself of the out-of-date "doctrine of shock"'.[4] What is more, he maintained that Russian reserve troops were less well-trained than their German counterparts and, unlike them, unfit to go straight into the line.

On 28 July 1914 the higher command appointments for the North-West Front, which would conduct the campaign in East Prussia with its two armies,

SWEDEN

Gotland

Öland

Baltic Sea

Riga

Memel

Königsberg

Danzig

**East Prussia**

Kovno

Vilna

XXXX 1
Rennenkampf

RUSSIAN

West Prussia

Marienburg

Suwalki

XXXX 8
Prittwitz

Tannenberg

Graudenz

Thorn

Grodno

Novgorodok

Minsk

XXXX 2
Samsonov

Lomza

Niemen

EMPIRE

GERMAN

Posen

Vistula

Novo Georgievsk

Bug

Brest-Litovsk

Pinsk

EMPIRE

Warth

Warsaw

Czersk

Poland

XXXX 9
Leschiski

Pripet
Marshes

Breslau

Ivangorod

XXXX 4
Salza

XXXX 5
Plehve

Silesia

XXXX
Kummer

Sandomierz

XXXX 3
Ruzski

Krakow

XXXX 1
Dankl

Przemysl

Galicia

XXXX 4
Auffenberg

Lemberg

Lvov

AUSTRO-

Kassa

XXXX
Kövess

XXXX 3
Brudermann

XXXX 2
Böhm Ermoli

Halicz

XXXX 8
Brussilov

Ukrain

HUNGARIAN

Vienna

EMPIRE

Carpathian

Mts

Czernowitz

Dniester

Budapest

Debrecen

from Serbia

Suceava

ROMANIA

were announced. As anticipated at the Kiev war games, General Zhilinski would conduct operations from his HQ in Bialystok, 40 miles from the nearest section of the East Prussian border and 50 miles south-west of Grodno. The commander of the First Army would be Rennenkampf (currently General Officer Commanding (GOC) Vilna Military District), the Second Army would be led by Samsonov (GOC Turkestan Military District).

In reality the armies destined to launch the invasion of East Prussia were only about 80 per cent of their nominal establishment, partly because guards had to be left at bridges and important installations vulnerable to sabotage by Poles and Lithuanians disenchanted with Russian rule. Furthermore, each artillery piece had a maximum of just 850 rounds when it went to war; an eventuality foreseen as early as 1912 but not rectified. A further administrative complication, which would become starkly evident in battle, concerned the many subordinate commanders through which the inadequate wireless and telephone systems must pass orders. Nor would supplies, ammunition and reinforcements easily reach the front line. In 1914 the Russian Army had just 679 self-propelled vehicles (of which reputedly only two were ambulances), with another 475 expected from civilian requisitions. Forward of the sparse railheads, all transport was horse-drawn; military formations were required to ride or march. The railways that did exist had low carrying capacity and were a different gauge to the German lines across the frontier.

**North East Europe, August 1914**

- **xxxx** Russian army
- **xxxx** German army
- **xxxx** Austro-Hungarian army
- defensive positions

Nevertheless, each of the two Russian armies in East Prussia with some 200,000 men would roughly equal the German Eighth Army opposing them. Together they should overwhelm the Germans, whose only chance of victory lay in beating Rennenkampf and Samsonov separately. Such a German success did not seem altogether far-fetched. Russian staff training was considered inadequate by other European nations, and Golovine reflected that Lieutenant General V.A. Sukhomlinov's appointment as Minister of War in 1909 represented ultra-conservatism: 'what he had learned decades ago was still unchangeably true'. Golovine condemned him as a product of 'an unhealthy organism ... the St Petersburg bureaucracy ... worse than an ignoramus, for besides this he was completely happy-go-lucky ... [and] inflicted incalculable harm upon the Russian Army'. His books and articles generally revealed Golovine as a jaundiced commentator. However, the Russian Foreign Minister (S.D. Sazonov) caustically observed of Sukhomlinov: 'It is very difficult to make him work but to get him to tell the truth was well-nigh impossible'.[5]

Brussilov was much less critical, providing a counter-weight to Golovine's entrenched bitterness. He believed Sukhomlinov's appointment as Minister of War to be advantageous, following fifteen years of administrative inertia under Nicholas II. Having served under Sukhomlinov, he held that 'he was undoubtedly a man of intelligence, a man who could grasp a situation and decide upon his course very rapidly'.[6] Brussilov believed that, bearing in mind the rudimentary Russian railway system and vast distances travelled by those called up, mobilization in 1914 went reasonably well. Nor could Sukhomlinov be blamed for another endemic weakness. The Russian Army – drawn as it was from an empire stretching over 5,000 miles west to east and from the Arctic to Afghanistan north to south – was not a homogeneous body. It comprised some 200 ethnic groupings, many of whose loyalty was so suspect that they were never posted to their own locality. The composition of these ethnic units was further diluted at the time of general mobilization by being brought up to strength with reservists from other minorities.

The different opinions of Sukhomlinov expressed by Golovine and Brussilov illuminated the factions which split the Russian military during the run-up to the First World War. Personally dissolute and not averse to financial inducement, the Minister of War was accused of appointing a succession of short-term Chiefs of the General Staff to minimize uniformed opposition to

**General Vladimir Aleksandrovich Sukhomlinov (1848–1926).**

As pre-war Russian War Minister sought to modernise the Russian Army but was baulked by entrenched military opposition. A debauched life-style and suspicion of his personal corruption did not help. Died in exile.

his office and seeking to destroy the fabric of the Russian Army through his radical plans for reorganization. He argued that obsolete frontier fortresses, which could be bypassed on railways and were vulnerable to modern artillery, should be decommissioned and the bloated cavalry establishment drastically pruned. A bevy of influential gunners and a 'cohort of cavalrymen'[7] combined to frustrate him: in 1914, for instance, the fortresses not only survived but commanded such a dominant share of the military budget that they contained 2,813 heavy guns, the field army only 240 heavy howitzers and cannon.

All Russian males (except the inhabitants of Finland, Mohammedans in the Caucasus and native populations in Asia) were liable for military service from the age of 20 to 43. Infantry served with the colours for three years, cavalry four. Depending on his arm, a soldier then spent fourteen or fifteen years in different elements of the reserve (requiring two training periods of six weeks) and a further five or six in the Opolchenie (militia); making a total commitment of twenty-three years. However, the training system could not cope with every eligible man, so liberal exceptions were allowed. Cossacks served for life, supplying their own horses and equipment. In July 1914 the Russian Army totalled 1,423,000 men. General mobilization would swell this number by 3,115,000 of trained reserves up to the age of 38. From these additional troops, 2 million would either reinforce existing formations or form new front-line units; the balance would go to depots or training establishments in the rear. The first-grade militia, aged 38 to 43, comprised about 800,000 men with at least some military training. In addition an indeterminate number of second-grade militia, exempt from service when called up at 20, had no military experience. The theoretical strength of the Russian Army at the end of August 1914 would, therefore, be approximately 6 million. However, as training for non-regulars was distinctly patchy, this imposing figure had little practical value. Nonetheless, the Russian Bear had the numerical potential for a lengthy campaign; the British military attaché, Brigadier General Knox, held that 15 million men were eligible for call-up; Russian official statistics show that 25 million men were of combat age in 1912.

**Cossacks on the march.** In August 1914, the Russian Army had 200,000 first-line Cossacks, with other second- and third-line reserves supporting infantry divisions. Both Russian army commanders during the East Prussian campaign led Cossacks in the Russo-Japanese War.

On mobilization, 192 depot battalions were formed to feed into front-line units. Knox drew particular attention to the low quality of many officers and NCOs. He also noted the number of rank and file unschooled in the technology of modern warfare; in 1914, 50 per cent being deemed illiterate. However, they did not lack raw courage, if well led. Unfortunately, in July 1914 even the peacetime establishment lacked 3,000 junior officers, requiring accelerated commissioning from military courses to fill vacancies. Nor was efficiency enhanced by the practice of appointing commanders down to regimental level from the privileged pool of General Staff and Imperial Guard officers. Many staff college graduates had never seen service in a regiment until posted to lead one, in extreme cases after twenty years in the army. Brussilov complained that 'irresponsible' selection boards gave 'undeserving candidates favourable reports' and the General Staff posted inadequate officers to army commands without revealing their professional shortcomings. As a result promotion for dedicated regimental officers was slow, with the over-

**War Bonds.**
All major partici-
pants in the First
World War raised
money through the
issue of War Bonds.
This poster was
part of the Russian
drive in 1914.

whelming majority failing to progress beyond major or, at best, lieutenant colonel. Brussilov concluded that in 1914 'technically our Army was very ill-prepared'.[8]

Whatever their administrative qualities, Russian senior commanders in 1914 did lack battle experience. Grand Duke Nikolai Nikolaievich was appointed Commander-in-Chief (C-in-C) of the Army on 2 August 1914. Required to execute war plans, which he had played no part in drawing up, he inherited staff officers that he had not chosen. His Chief of Staff, Yanushkevich, until recently CGS, had never seen active service nor commanded more than a company; the press welcomed his elevation to such an important post with less than wild enthusiasm. Much of his career had been spent as a staff officer in the Ministry of War; his appointment as Chief of Staff resulted more from Imperial patronage than proven fighting ability. Brussilov agreed that his appointment was 'fatal … an agreeable man, [but] he was rather irresolute and a poor strategist'.[9]

**Grand Duke Nikolai Nikolaievich**

General Zhilinski, 61-year-old commander of the North-West Front, had some active service. He held a staff appointment during the Russo-Japanese War, then led a cavalry division in Poland. As CGS, 1910–13, he represented Russia during the decisive staff conferences in August 1913 which determined Franco-Russian strategy in the event of war with Germany. Briefly commander of the Warsaw Military District, at the outbreak of war he was appointed to the North-West Front despite his comparative lack of field experience. Reputedly he was unpopular with subordinates. The British military attaché, acknowledging Zhilinski to be 'generally unpopular', thought him 'an official of the cut-and-dried type'.[10]

General Pavel (Paul) Karlovich von Rennenkampf, a 60-year-old from a noble family and graduate of the Nikolaievski Military Academy, had secured rapid promotion to major general at the age of 46. He commanded a cavalry column during the Boxer Rising of 1900 and a division of Trans-Baikal Cossacks in the Russo-Japanese War, from which he emerged with a reputation in Russia for energy and ability. Foreign observers, including a German

**General Pavel (Paul) Karlovich von Rennenkampf (1853–1918),** commander of the Russian First Army (second left) dining with his staff at Insterburg during the East Prussian campaign. Unpopular with subordinates, he was eventually shot by the Bolsheviks.

general attached to the Japanese army, were less sure of Rennenkampf, criticizing both his handling of cavalry and, particularly, lax reconnaissance. *The Times* military correspondent, Charles à C. Repington, dismissed his so-called reconnaissance activity in north-east Korea as 'an aimless ramble'; in general 'the Russian horsemen were headless' during the campaign.[11] Kuropatkin praised Rennenkampf's courage; he was wounded in action and fought in numerous encounters including the battles of Shaho river and Mukden. He frequently took control of all-arm detachments, in one action totalling 60,000 rifles, 6,000 sabres, 200 guns and 1,500 engineers. Rennenkampf subsequently served as a corps commander for eight years, during which he vigorously suppressed dissident, but lightly armed, rebels in Siberia until appointed to command the Vilna Military District in 1913. Like Zhilinski he was not popular with subordinates, and, reportedly, rarely spoke to his own chief of staff after appointment to the First Army in 1914.

General Alexander Vasilievich Samsonov, aged 55, had joined a cavalry regiment when 18, seen service in Turkey during the 1877 crisis, then attended the Nikolaievski Military Academy. Promoted major general at 43, he commanded a cavalry school in the 1890s and, like Rennenkampf, a cavalry unit during the Boxer Rising. He led successively a cavalry brigade then a division of Siberian Cossacks in the Russo-Japanese War, being admired by the Russians for his dashing performance in sweeps and raids. But foreign observers doubted his ability in set battles like Mukden, pointing to lack of strategic acumen and, again like Rennenkampf, a rudimentary grasp of the principles of reconnaissance. A likeable man, but a poor general was the British and German verdict. After the Russo-Japanese War he served as Chief of Staff to the Warsaw Military District, then GOC Turkestan Military District, where he remained until appointed to the Second Army. He knew in advance that this would be his role in the event of hostilities; but many of his staff did not. Thus they were neither prepared for nor experienced in working with one another. Samsonov, an asthma sufferer, was on sick leave when mobilization commenced and did not reach his HQ until 12 August. Knox, who had observed him on pre-war manoeuvres, wrote that Samsonov had 'a simple, kindly nature, and his staff were all devoted to him'. But he thought his experience 'a poor preparation for the command of a large army in modern war'.[12]

**General Alexander Vasilievich Samsonov (1859–1914),** commander of the Russian Second Army during the battle of Tannenberg. Led cavalry during the Boxer Rising and Russo-Japanese War, gaining a reputation for daring action. Popular with his men, but critics who doubted his strategic ability were vindicated in East Prussia. Committed suicide.

## GERMAN FORCES

With very few exceptions, all men were liable for military service between the ages of 17 and 45, although physical entry into the German Army did not take place until 20. The initial seven years active service in regular then reserve units (a ratio of 2:5 for infantry, 3:4 for cavalry) was followed by reserve service

**Mobilization, August 1914:** German troops prepare to march. Including regular and reserve formations of all arms, on paper Germany mobilized four million, Russia six million men.

requiring two training periods of eight weeks. Men then went to the Landwehr (territorial reserve) for eleven years – the first five of which entailed annual training – and finally six years in the local defence Landsturm, whose principal role was protection of the homeland. The peace establishment of the regular German Army was some 800,000 men, with an additional 1 million in reserve units. The Landwehr totalled approximately 1.5 million, the Landsturm another 800,000; making a grand total of some 4 million men.

The Kaiser was nominally C-in-C of the German armed forces, though in practice the Army CGS (Moltke) issued orders on his behalf from GHQ. The General Staff provided trained officers for all formations from divisions upwards. The German officer corps was no longer an aristocratic preserve, yet promotion to command a division normally took forty years. Advancement

resulted from annual reports and inspections, not a
formal examination. Staff College selection occurred
after nine years' regimental service, which meant that
all officers did have at least junior command experience. The Germans had developed mechanized
transport during peacetime and practised absorbing
requisitioned civilian vehicles in time of war. In this
respect they were far more prepared than the
Russians. Lieutenant General Vasili Iosifovich Gurko,
who led the 1st Cavalry Division in East Prussia,
recalled: 'When my cavalry came into contact with
the Germans, they could always see, following the
enemy, long columns of motor transport of different
types filled with troops'.[13]

At the outbreak of war, East Prussia was defended
by the German I Infantry Corps, which was absorbed
into the Eighth Army whose complement of regular,
reserve and Landwehr formations was then equivalent to eleven and a half
infantry divisions and one cavalry division. In addition, troops assigned to the
defence of Königsberg and other East Prussian fortifications effectively made
up another division, and perhaps the equivalent of a further division were
close by in West Prussia, stationed at fortresses like Graudenz and Thorn. With
this force, the Eighth Army commander (66-year-old General Maximilian von
Prittwitz und Gaffron) must defend both East and West Prussia. Prittwitz, a
soldier for forty-nine years, had fought in the Austro-Prussian and Franco-
Prussian wars, gained an Iron Cross (Second Class) and had held general rank
for over seventeen years. In East Prussia, he was ordered to avoid being overwhelmed in the field or being driven to take refuge in Königsberg. Lieutenant
Colonel C.A.M. (Max) Hoffmann, his 45-year-old principal staff officer, drew
attention to further instructions to retire west of the Vistula 'in the event of
the advance of greatly superior Russian forces', which 'contained great psycho-

**General Helmuth
Johannes Ludwig
von Moltke (1848–
1916), 'the
Younger'.** As Chief
of the German
General Staff,
Moltke modified the
Schlieffen Plan to
avoid violating
Dutch neutrality and
strengthened the
left (southern) wing
contrary to
Schlieffen's inten-
tions.

logical dangers for weak characters'. Hoffmann did not include Prittwitz, 'a clever, though somewhat harsh superior' whom he knew well, in this category.[14] He was less sure of Major General Count von Waldersee, Prittwitz's Chief of Staff, 'a highly educated and able officer … [whose] physical powers were not equal to his mental' and whose 'nerves were still suffering' from the effects of a serious operation. Hoffmann himself had served for lengthy periods in Prussia, 'which became like a second home to me', attended the German Staff College, qualified as a Russian interpreter, spent six months in Russia and five years in the Russian Department of the Great General Staff. On 7 August he wrote in his diary: 'We have a hard task before us, harder almost than any in history … I confidently hope that we shall be able to deal with it'.[15]

## EAST PRUSSIA

After the elimination of Poland as a separate political entity in 1795, its rump then being divided between Prussia, Russia and Austria, East Prussia was effectively a salient protruding into Russian territory, its base along the Baltic coast curved roughly clockwise from Memel in the north to Elbing in the south-west. Just 100 miles at its widest, west–east, it stretched a maximum 160 miles north to south, although its border adjoining Russia was by no means regular. Immediately south of Memel, the long river bearing its name (but called the Niemen in Russia) flowed into the sea; the smaller Pregel river did so at Königsberg. Close to Gumbinnen 70 miles east of Königsberg, the Angerapp tributary ran into the Pregel; 20 miles east of Königsberg the Alle river similarly flowed 90 miles south to north into the Pregel. The 60 mile long Masurian Lakes complex lay approximately north–south from 20 miles south of Gumbinnen to a point close to the southern frontier. The province's western border meandered north from the Soldau river, along the side of prominent lakes, east of Marienburg and Elbing to the Baltic Sea. Behind it the Vistula river ran parallel through West Prussia, reaching the Baltic east of Danzig. Any withdrawal to that line would therefore entail the surrender of East Prussia to the Russians. Königsberg provided a valuable seaport through

**Lieutenant Colonel C.A.M. (Max) Hoffmann (1869–1927).** Principal staff officer to the German Eighth Army during the East Prussian campaign under both Prittwitz and Hindenburg. Credited by some sources with the plan decisively to transfer troops southwards before the battle of Tannenberg.

which reinforcements and supplies could be brought. Between the major lakes and rivers, the terrain was yet further pockmarked by a multitude of smaller ponds and sheets of water, especially in a 40 mile swathe parallel to the southern frontier.

Railways would be decisive in any military campaign. In the north-east, a double-track line from Vilna in Russia to Königsberg crossed the border at Eydtkuhnen; close to the south-eastern bulge of the frontier, 40 miles from Eydtkuhnen, ran the single track from Suwalki to Marggrabowa. Piercing the southern frontier were two more single tracks, Grajewo–Lyck and Kolno–Johannisburg, 30 miles apart, the former 25 miles from the Suwalki line. The western extremity of the southern frontier had the double-track from Warsaw to Soldau via Mlawa, 55 miles from the Kolno crossing. These access tracks for the Russians into East Prussia were, therefore, widely dispersed and suffered from the great disadvantage that the Russian and German track gauges were different. Within East Prussia the Germans enjoyed a comprehensive honeycomb of railways, with numerous spurs leading off three lengthy double-track lines: running roughly south-west to north-east from Deutsch-Eylau to Insterburg; due east from Königsberg across the Russian frontier; south-west along the Baltic coast from Königsberg to Marienburg.

In essence, for defensive purposes East Prussia could be divided into geographical sections. Königsberg was actually a fortified arc, based on the Baltic coast, bulging 20 miles eastwards to Tapiau and arching from the coastal town of Labiau 25 miles north-east to Brandenburg, 20 miles south-west. With strong outworks to supplement the elderly inner fortifications, this formidable defensive position would sit uneasily on the flank of any attacking force which attempted to bypass it for Berlin. Some 30 miles east of Tapiau, from the railway junction of Insterburg 40 miles south to Angerburg abutting the Masurian Lakes, stood the vulnerable Insterburg Gap – a plain dotted with forests and marshes; the Angerapp river was fordable and the whole area liable to penetration by determined attackers. The Masurian Lakes from Angerapp to Johannisburg, pierced only by narrow defiles, were more promising for defenders who could deploy undetected behind their screen. The fourth area comprised the 75 mile common frontier with Russian Poland from Johannisburg in the east to Soldau in the west. South of the frontier, the deliberate policy of non-development had made the terrain into a desert and virtual wasteland which would slow a potential invader. In Prussia, though, the roads were passable, the countryside cultivated, and well-stocked villages flourished. On the other hand, apart from a stretch west of Neidenburg, wooded country benefited the defenders. Although the Germans were inferior in force levels, natural obstacles thus favoured the defence. Lateral movement from east to west, and to some extent also south to north, would be hampered by the many rivers and lakes. Nevertheless, weaknesses lay north and west of the Masurian Lakes. The German strategist Karl von Clausewitz would have expected a Russian concentration on one of these points to maximize the superior forces at their disposal. Zhilinski opted for a different approach.

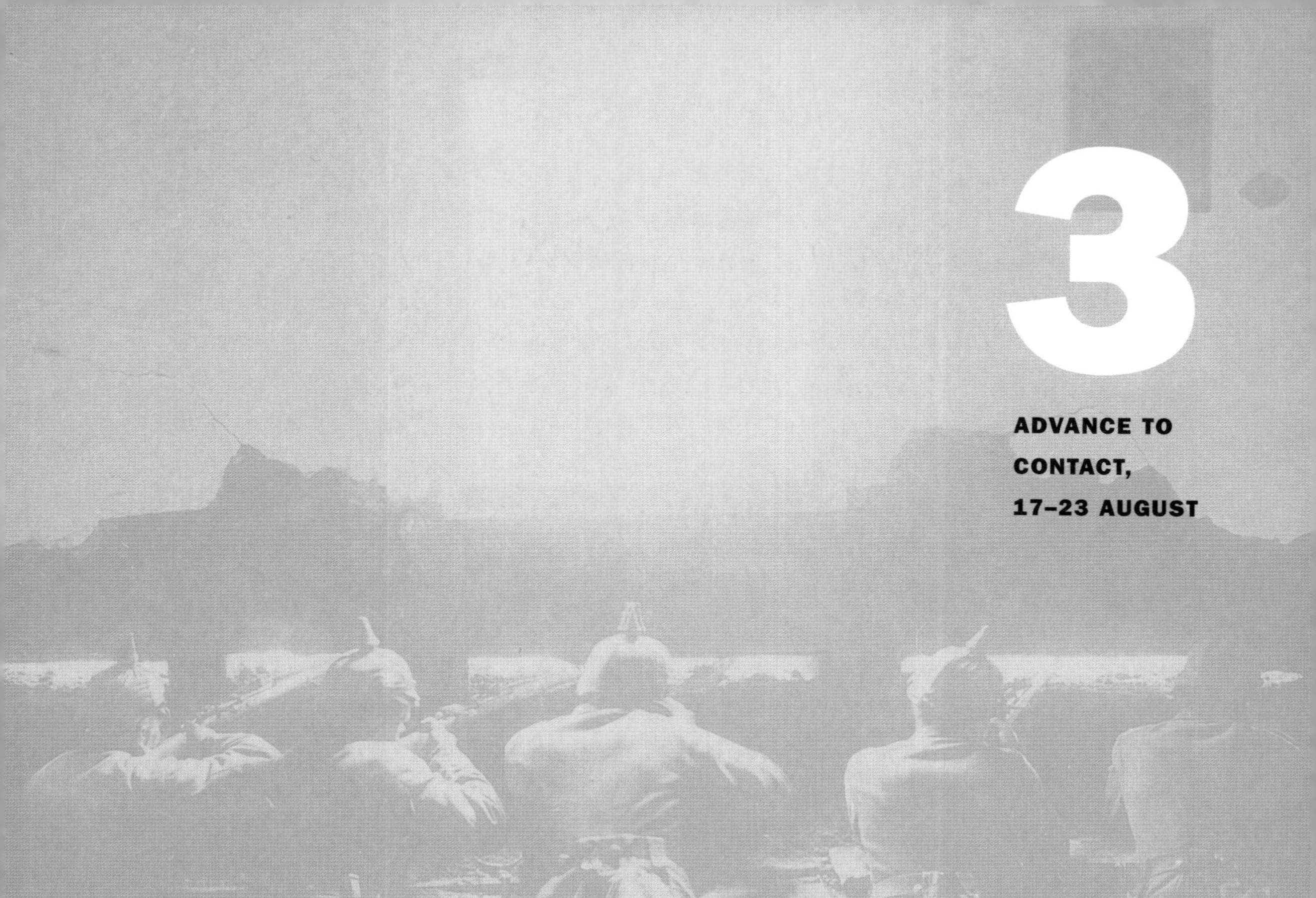

**ADVANCE TO
CONTACT,
17–23 AUGUST**

## RUSSIAN PLANS

In Russia, while reservists converged on military depots and staff officers pored over the administrative minutiae of war, a wave of patriotism stifled political unrest. Brigadier General A.W.F. Knox, the British military attaché, commented on the 'wonderful August days of 1914' in St Petersburg (soon to be renamed Petrograd), where enthusiastic crowds thronged the streets and squares, strikers returned to work and church services lauded the coming fight to protect civilization from a rampant Germany; 'as if we were going to the Crusades' in the words of tsarist officer Pavel Rodzianko.[1] On 30 July in Warsaw, though, General A.A. Brussilov reported all quiet, 'clearly the public had no idea that we were on the eve of war'. That day General Baron von Traubenberg of the Warsaw District staff assured him that 'everyone was satisfied that we should have no war'. Two days later 'came Armageddon, but none could imagine its magnitude or its consequences', Brussilov reflected.[2]

Two military options had been drawn up in case of war. Plan G, if the Germans and Austrians attacked Russia, foresaw the First, Second and Fourth armies in the north-west to cope with any threat from East Prussia; the Third and Fourth armies further south opposing Austria–Hungary; the Sixth and Seventh armies in reserve. Plan A envisaged Germany concentrating on France, which would trigger Russia's treaty obligations. Then, the First and Second armies would invade East Prussia, with Third, Fourth and Fifth armies attacking Austria–Hungary; the Sixth and Seventh armies again in reserve. Plan A was a diluted version of Plan 19 drawn up in 1910, which allocated four armies to attack East Prussia, with the Austro-Hungarian front a secondary theatre.

The German invasion of Belgium on 4 August provoked immediate discussion about the focus of Russian deployment. For some time the French General Staff had been convinced that the main German blow would fall in the west. Despite her previous undertakings, however, Russia procrastinated. On 5 August the French ambassador M. Maurice Paléologue addressed an impassioned plea to the tsar: 'The French Army will be forced to withstand the powerful onslaught of twenty-five German corps. I therefore implore Your Majesty to order your armies to take an immediate offensive. If they do not, there is a danger that the French Army will be crushed'. The following day, Yanushkevich signalled Zhilinski to 'prepare for an energetic offensive against Germany at the earliest possible moment … [though] only when sufficient strength has been made available'.[3] Plan A would be implemented. To build on anticipated success, a new army (ready by 26 August) would be formed to advance on the left of Second Army and co-operate with the North-West Front in its drive towards Berlin. To achieve the first phase of this operation, East Prussia would be occupied.

On 8 August GHQ informed Zhilinski that the Guard and I corps would be withdrawn from his First Army and sent to Warsaw; replaced only by the XX Corps. Two days later, after the North–West Front commander's own plans had been rejected by GHQ, Yanushkevich issued more detailed instructions on behalf of Grand Duke Nikolai. With the XIII Corps not yet ready, the Russian First Army would comprise the III and IV corps, six regiments from the XX Corps, the 5th Rifle Brigade and five and a half cavalry divisions. The Second Army was to consist of the II, VI, XV and XXIII corps, the 1st Rifle Brigade and four cavalry divisions; from these, two divisions and the 1st Rifle Brigade might be detached to Novo Georgievsk for protection of the lines of communication with Warsaw. Both armies were to concentrate by the evening of 11 August. Yanushkevich explained: 'It is our duty to support France in view of the great stroke prepared by Germany against her'.

'Drawing upon itself the greatest possible enemy strength ... with calm minds and trusting in God', the First Army would advance north of the Masurian Lakes and turn the German left flank; the Second Army go round the south of the Lakes aiming to destroy the Germans between them and the Vistula and preventing other enemy forces reaching that river. 'The closest liaison must be maintained between the First and Second armies' with both prepared to move by 13 August, even though their rear echelons were not due for completion until 19 August.

After reading the specific orders relating to destruction of German units west of the Masurian Lakes, on 12 August Zhilinski wired his intention to extend his line westwards from Lomja to Chorzele for 'a greater strategic effect', and Yanushkevich concurred. It was now obvious that neither army would meet the starting target of 13 August. In fact, also on 12 August, Zhilinski pointed out to GHQ that the First Army's cavalry could not cross the border in strength before 15 August, advanced bodies of infantry 18–19 August; the main body of the Second Army could not do so until 19 August at the earliest.[4]

Zhilinski did not issue his orders to the two army commanders until 13 August. 'I propose to embark on a determined offensive with the object of defeating the enemy, cutting him off from Königsberg, and seizing his lines of retreat upon the Vistula', he declared. He required Rennenkampf to send his cavalry 'supported by infantry detachments' across the frontier on the

**Brussels, August 1914.** German artillery passing through the Belgian capital as part of the Schlieffen Plan to defeat France before attacking Russia.

**Russian General Headquarters, Baranovichi.** Accompanied by Nikolaievich's chief of staff, Lieutenant General N.N. Yanushkevich, Belgian and French military representatives inspect a Russian guard of honour.

morning of 16 August 'to drive in the enemy's advanced units, and to consolidate the positions occupied'. All three First Army corps would invade East Prussia on 17 August 'the first objective being the front Insterburg–Angerburg, the offensive to be developed to turn the enemy's left flank'. Particular care must be taken to maintain 'a screen opposite Lötzen, from which direction a German offensive may be expected'. The right flank (II) corps of the Second Army would advance from Augustow over the frontier on 19 August, aiming towards Lyck, Arys and Lötzen. Zhilinski reminded his two army commanders that 'the enemy must, in all cases, be attacked energetically and with the greatest determination'.[5]

In a separate instruction Zhilinski required the Second Army to advance north-westwards behind (west of) the Masurian Lakes, deploy the II Corps to cover the line Grodno–Augustow and guard against a German assault on its left flank from the direction of Allenstein. His evaluation of the German strength and dispositions revealed intelligence deficiencies, which would haunt the Russians throughout the coming weeks. He estimated that only two corps, supported by an unknown number of reservist and Landwehr personnel, were in the field; German advanced guards on the frontier with the main force behind the Masurian Lakes. To complete the southern envelopment of the German Eighth Army, the Russian Second Army should send its cavalry over the frontier on 18 August followed by the main body the following day. Zhilinski urged both armies to press ahead rapidly during their first two days in East Prussia 'in order to ascertain what forces the enemy has at its disposal'. To his cavalry the North-West Front commander gave 'the task of screening and hiding from the enemy the direction of march of our Corps, the consolidation of specially important points, the seizing of crossings, and the penetrating far in the rear of the enemy in order to prevent the removal of rolling stock from the railways'.[6]

Zhilinski recognized the importance of quickly seizing control of the German railways and, even more critically, the rolling stock capable of carrying men and equipment on the different gauge (German 4ft 8.5ins; Russian 5ft). However, passage of men and fighting *matériel* took precedence on the railway between Kovno and Verjbolow at the frontier, so the planned track conversion equipment could not in the event be quickly brought up. The necessary orders were issued to their subordinate formations by the Second (14 August) and the First Army (15 August). Both armies still lacked essential military supplies and, even more critically, food – so that living off the land became commonplace, especially for the Second Army, which had totally inadequate transport support. On 3 August the 4th Cavalry Division probed across the frontier ahead of the Second Army to discover that German troops had abandoned areas east of Lyck and around Bialla, where evidence of occupation by the German XX Corps was reported. At the western extremity of Samsonov's line, on 6 August north-west of Chorzele the 6th and

Чтожъ, теперь узнаешъ вкусъ.
Потяну тебя за усъ,
Чтобъ не думалъ о Руси,
На, щелчкомъ ты закуси.
А союзникъ твой, австріецъ,
Этотъ жадный кровопіецъ,
На колѣни сѣлъ отъ страха
И поползъ какъ черепаха.

Собствен. изданіе
ФАБРИКИ
А. Ф. Постнова
Перепечатка воспрещ.

Дозв. Цензурою 12 авгус. 1914 г.

**Russian cartoon.**
A Russian soldier lifts Wilhelm II by his ears as his Austro-Hungarian ally, Franz Joseph I, cowers below. The soldier berates Wilhelm for underestimating Russian and overestimating Austrian power.

15th Cavalry divisions swept the Soldau/Neidenburg region, reputedly ripping up 3 miles of railway track, blowing up viaducts and destroying the station at Schlafken. They were later accused of wantonly burning villages and ejecting their inhabitants. Units of the German XVII Corps were identified near Neidenburg; further west part of the 15th Cavalry Division encountered detachments advancing from the fortress of Thorn. Evidence of the German I Corps and 1st Cavalry Division were also uncovered by the Russian 2nd Cavalry Division scouting in front of Rennenkampf. Knox was therefore wrong to dub these excursions 'of little importance'. Golovine held, more reasonably, that before 17 August 'everything was done by it [the cavalry] … under the conditions of 1914'.[7]

## GERMAN DEFENCES

In East Prussia, on the first day of the war, Landsturm personnel began to man sensitive frontier positions; the German I Corps threw forward troops to Eydtkuhnen on the eastern border with other units behind at Insterburg; a Landwehr brigade replaced front-line troops at Memel. The Germans sent cavalry patrols into Russian-held Poland between Kalisch and Benzin shortly after the declaration of war, though these were too far west to secure any valuable information about Russian deployments. However, the intention and to a large extent plans of the Russians were already known, as Russian wireless operators usually transmitted without encrypting their messages. Hoffmann brushed aside the staff's suspicion that these insecure transmissions were a Russian ruse. When a belated crude cipher came into use on 26 August, even that was quickly broken. Prittwitz, therefore, was well aware that the First and Second armies intended to meet west of the Masurian Lakes following a double envelopment movement. His staff fairly accurately predicted that the Russians would advance between 15 and 20 August using troops already stationed close to the frontier, leaving reserves to protect the lines of communication. Reinforcements for the two field armies would take 'a considerable time' to arrive, though, giving opportunity for the Eighth Army to attack whichever

**Battle of Tannenberg.** Advancing across the southern
border of East Prussia, the Russian Second Army was lured
towards strong German defensive positions, which delayed
its progress until arrival of reinforcements from the north.
These German infantry occupy a fortified farmhouse.

of the Russian armies took the field first. Hoffmann estimated, rightly, that this would be the army advancing from Vilna, because that from Warsaw 'would have to make its way through a district near our frontier that was both boggy and deficient in roads'.[8]

Like the Russians, the Germans had conducted preparatory war games, paying particular attention to the narrow defiles between the Masurian Lakes, where a number of fortifications had been constructed – the strongest at the most vulnerable point, Lötzen. During the morning of 14 August Prittwitz received reports that the Russians were on the move towards Marggrabowa, but that all was quiet in the Vladislvov/Vishtinets (Wyschtinjetz) sector. The roads leading west from Mariampol and Kavariya were empty, but cavalry had been identified in the Verjbolow area.

The German line-up in East Prussia at the beginning of August 1914 comprised the six infantry divisions of the I, XVII and XX corps; three divisions of the I Reserve Corps; Landwehr (territorial reserve) units equivalent in total to five divisions; the 1st Cavalry Division. The Germans expanded their reserve corps from pre-war cadres and manned their fortresses with Landwehr, whose ability the Russians seriously underestimated. The local defence Landsturm troops, too, were much more effective than the Russian militia, being used to guard forty-five frontier points within the German I Corps area. Assuming that Rennenkampf would indeed move first, at 4 p.m. on 14 August Prittwitz issued his deployment orders with the bulk of his troops set to oppose the Russian First Army. He laid down specific instructions about aerial observation, which indicated that he had a greater grasp of its strategic and tactical importance than Zhilinski. Emphasizing that control of the air service rested with individual corps, he required the XX Corps to provide aerial reconnaissance 'to the River Narew and beyond'; the I Corps 'to the River Niemen and via Tilsit to Shavli'. Cover should be provided, too, for detachments at Strasburg, Lautenburg, Soldau and Neidenburg. Airship Section No. 8 was to transfer to Nordenburg and come under the I Corps. To avoid administrative confusion the Eighth Army commander then laid down clear, separate lines of communication for each corps. Prittwitz closed his orders by announcing that Army HQ would move from Marienburg to Bartenstein by midday 16 August. Hoffmann rather edgily mused: 'If it comes off, Prittwitz will be a great commander, if it does not we shall get into trouble … The responsibility is gigantic'. Pessimistically, he added: 'Waldersee is rather weak. I hope he will not let us down at the last moment'.[9]

## RUSSIAN FIRST ARMY ON THE MOVE

Meanwhile, Rennenkampf had not been idle. On 6 August, soon after his 2nd Cavalry Division (Lieutenant General Nahichevanski) penetrated East Prussian territory further north, the 1st Cavalry Division (Lieutenant General Gurko) and 5th Rifle Brigade gathered at Suwalki to begin exploring across the border. Patrols into enemy territory soon discovered Germans in the area of Marggrabowa, but to Gurko's displeasure failed either to blow up sections of nearby railway lines as ordered or ride further afield towards Goldap. The First Army commander then ordered Gurko to establish more thoroughly the strength of the German forces in front of him. Thus on 12 August Cornet V.S. Littauer of the Russian 1st Hussars found himself in the frontier village of Bakalarjevo, where 'the border was a narrow ditch, winding through pleasant pastoral country'. He took the opportunity to join a small band which briefly and unofficially rode into East Prussia. 'The war was not yet real … We were like children playing "hide and seek" certain (and half way hoping) we were going to be discovered at any moment'. They were not the first to make an unscheduled incursion, coming across a Russian infantry soldier returning unconcernedly to Russian territory with a heavy load of stolen German geese.[10]

'Our romantic attitude was soon shattered', Littauer reflected. On the evening of 12 August Gurko gathered his whole cavalry division and, supported by a light infantry regiment, advanced on Marggrabowa, 7 miles away. As he was preparing to move off, Littauer noticed one squadron commander remove his cap and cross himself. 'I looked round and saw that all the men were also crossing themselves. Just to be on the safe side, I did so too'. While the cavalry negotiated dusty tracks in the darkness, the flanking infantry crossed open terrain communicating by simulated bird calls. At dawn on 13 August, confronted by the approaching Russian force, a small German advance unit took refuge in a copse, pursued by dismounted cavalry. As whistling noises and sounds of impact on the closely packed tree trunks were heard, Littauer mused: 'I suppose they are bullets'; his first time in action.[11] Having brushed aside this minor, military irritant, at 7 a.m. the Russian 1st Cavalry Division breasted a hill to see Marggrabowa immediately ahead 'in rolling open country', protected by numerous little lakes. Supported by field artillery, the Russian infantry and dismounted Russian cavalry inched their way along the narrow fingers of land between the lakes; 'the lake isthmuses over which were the macadamised roads leading to Marggrabowa', according to Gurko. Littauer described the distant scene. 'From where we were it all looked like a war game … The knowledge that we were witnessing people killing each other penetrated neither my brain nor heart'. Although the defenders resisted only relatively briefly, several casualties were suffered including the unlucky Captain Lazarev, killed while his mare 'was munching hay from a stack'. More generally, Littauer noted that 'the scene on the German side of the border was quite frightening. For miles, farms, haystacks and barns were burning'. He later dismissed claims that Russian troops had caused this carnage. Independently, Gurko agreed. He pointed to the sight of fleeing cyclists, which suggested that the fires were the unprompted work of local youths; for many farms were untouched, tethered animals and half-eaten meals in some houses testimony to hasty departures. 'We had to order these young cyclists to be fired on. Thereafter they showed themselves much less frequently', Gurko drily observed.[12] After confirming that the German troops had abandoned Marggrabowa, gleaning further information from the telegraph office and dismantling military installations, the Russians withdrew over the border once more to await arrival of Rennenkampf's main force, suspecting that innocent-looking civilians were reporting their progress. Gurko noted that 'several times we captured German soldiers dressed as peasants, and even as women', the latter disguise being betrayed 'by the Government underclothing they wore'.[13]

Still on Russian soil, the First Army had been hampered by non-arrival of reserve troops marooned along the inadequate, interior railway system, and the need to post guards (sometimes of company strength) to protect rear areas. Nonetheless, from Vilna on 15 August Rennenkampf issued a directive for the First Army to cross the frontier two days later. Summarizing the preamble to Zhilinski's orders, he required it to advance from the line Vladislvov–Suwalki to Insterburg–Angerburg, preparatory to turning the line at the Masurian Lakes from the north.

**Stalluponen, August 1914.** Russian troops after capture of the railway junction five miles inside the East Prussia border on 17 August 1914. Note the damage caused to the building by artillery shells.

More detailed instructions later that same day made the infantry divisions nominally responsible for scouting with their own attached second- and third-line Cossack squadrons, few of which had actually arrived. In their absence, therefore, most infantry divisions had a detached squadron from a front-line cavalry division; but these were numerically inadequate. So the Russian infantry in effect advanced blindly. In contrast, each German infantry division had its own dedicated cavalry regiment. At 3 a.m. on 17 August Rennenkampf established his HQ behind the III Corps. Technically the First Army had fulfilled Russia's political commitment, by beginning to march from its concentration area on 14 August (the fifteenth day of mobilization).

Desultory small arms exchanges during the preceding night foreshadowed the bulk of the First Army crossing into East Prussia on 17 August, though Army HQ did not closely timetable the operation. At each individual commander's initiative, on the right the XX Corps, less the 116th Regiment, began to do so at noon; in the centre, the III Corps had already crossed between 8 and 9 a.m.; on the left the IV Corps took between 11 a.m. and 2 p.m. to complete its invasion.

By 11 a.m., under fire from German heavy artillery, the III Corps was engaged along the line Eydtkuhnen–Budweitschen. An attempt by German infantry to outflank its right-hand unit, the 25th Division, was foiled. Then

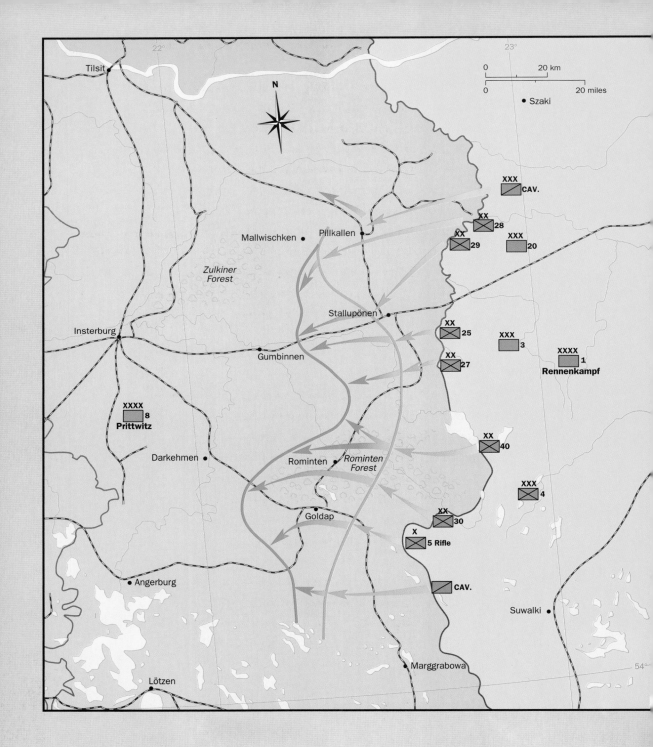

Tilsit

22°

N

Szaki

23°

0    20 km

0    20 miles

XXX
CAV.

XX
28

Mallwischken    Pillkallen

XX
29        XXX
20

Zulkiner
Forest

Stallupönen

XX
25        XXX
3

Insterburg

Gumbinnen    XX
27        XXXX
1
Rennenkampf

XXXX
8
Prittwitz

Darkehmen

Rominten    Rominten
Forest        XX
40

XXX
4

Goldap        XX
30

X
5 Rifle

Angerburg        CAV.

Suwalki

Lötzen        Marggrabowa        54°

the 29th Division adjacent to it on the XX Corps' left cleared the III Corps' northern flank by driving back German infantry at Bildersweitschen, capturing a number of prisoners and eight guns. Further south, on the III Corps' left, the IV Corps came under strong pressure as the Germans exploited a 12 mile gap between its right-hand 40th Division and the 27th Division of the III Corps. Lack of Russian cavalry in close support proved critical. The German 2nd Division hit both the Russian infantry divisions on the flank and rear, causing particular havoc in the 105th Orenburgski Regiment of the 27th Division, whose commander was killed, a total of 31 officers and 2,989 men casualties or missing. Still further south, only minor clashes occurred; on the Russian right, Nahichevanski's Cavalry Corps had pushed forward with little trouble.

## EXCHANGES AT STALLUPÖNEN

The major confrontation of 17 August took place when the XX Corps encountered forward elements of the German I Corps 5 miles inside the border at Stallupönen, an important railway junction east of Gumbinnen. The opening battle of the East Prussian campaign ensued. With no time to entrench and the action not preceded by artillery bombardment, a series of unconnected skirmishes developed involving heavy local casualties: the Russian III Corps lost an estimated 3,000 men mainly to machine gun fire, and many others fled from the field. According to Hoffmann, Prittwitz was furious that General Herman von Francois, commander of the I Corps, had given battle and risked any casualties; the Germans could ill afford anything like these losses. Having confirmed that the main Russian thrust was north of the Lakes, Prittwitz had intended the I Corps to retire. Before the battle, however, the Eighth Army and I Corps commanders had sharply disagreed. Francois, who was in charge of the corps providing long-term protection to East Prussia, argued that no violation of the province's territory should be tolerated. He wanted to take aggressive action along the border to drive back

**Russian First Army, 17–20 August**

| | |
|---|---|
| XXX | Russian army unit |
| XXXX | German army unit |
| ← | Russian attack |
| — | Russian front line 18 August |
| — | Russian front line 20 August |

potential invaders, which would effectively divorce him from the rest of the Eighth Army. 'To his great astonishment' on 17 August Waldersee learned that Francois had therefore marched beyond his ordered position, leading to the unplanned clash at Stallupönen. Prittwitz angrily ordered Francois by telephone and telegraph to obey instructions, not to squander men at his own whim, and to concentrate in the Gumbinnen/Insterburg area. Francois affected a Nelsonian indifference – not for the last time during the campaign. At 1 p.m. Prittwitz's QMG (Major General Grünert) was dispatched by car to exert discipline over this 'high-handed action'.[14] According to his own later claim, the volatile Francois sent him away with the proverbial flea in his ear: 'Report to General Prittwitz that General Francois will break off the engagement when he has defeated the Russians'; rank insubordination, if true. Hoffmann implies that Francois did obey Grünert, but undoubtedly reinforcements from both the Corps' 1st and 2nd divisions were still being committed during the afternoon. Francois incurred so many casualties during the day, especially on his left flank which he constantly strengthened, that he had no alternative but to withdraw westwards that evening. There seems scant evidence, therefore, that he did obey Prittwitz's order delivered by Grünert. Hoffmann admitted that Francois had successfully faced superior forces and taken 'many thousands of prisoners', but insisted that 'with regard to the general position, it [Stallupönen] was a mistake'.[15] The Russians suffered 63 officer and 6,664 other rank casualties to an estimated total of 1,000 for the Germans. Lack of Russian artillery and cavalry close support had been palpably obvious.

Although the Russian XX and IV corps did make satisfactory progress on 17 August, the reverses suffered by III Corps in the centre meant that Rennenkampf had to send out revised orders for 18 August. Needing vitally to reorganize, many units did not move forward again until around 2 p.m. Still the bulk of the cavalry were stationed on the flanks with few available to scout in front of the infantry. When they did so, communications were so unreliable that information had often to pass laboriously through the First

Army HQ to the corps. The Germans were content to draw Rennenkampf forward, but the Russian commander displayed no urgency to advance. By the evening of 18 August the First Army had reached a line some 45 miles long running roughly north–south through Stallupönen, scarcely 10 miles inside the frontier. On the right (northern) flank, Nahichevanski's Cavalry Corps (now four divisions plus eight field batteries) were at Pillkalen, having overcome a curious collection of dismounted cavalry and cyclists on the way; the XX north of Stallupönen; the III Corps immediately to the south; the IV Corps had penetrated the Rominten Forest; Gurko's 1st Cavalry Division and the 5th Rifle Brigade were on the extreme left (southern) flank.

The Russian advance towards Gumbinnen resumed on 19 August, though orders from the First Army HQ reached some corps in a garbled fashion. Rennenkampf aimed to reach the line Ushbalen–Puspern–Sodehnen–Goldap that day, which included reaching the east bank of the Rominte river. The Cavalry Corps in the north, learning that during the morning the 2nd Landwehr Brigade had been sent from Tilsit by train to Szillen and was marching towards Kraupischken to harass the Russian right flank, independently took the offensive. Riding north-west, the 1st and 2nd Guard divisions dismounted and supported by six field artillery batteries drove the Germans back across the Inster river, as the 3rd Regiment of Lifeguards executed a classic cavalry charge to capture two guns. Nahichevanski then bivouacked for the night, without seizing or destroying bridges over the river on the grounds that 'the ominous darkness, the fire maintained on the right bank by several German units, and the fact that the ammunition supply was exhausted, made pursuit out of the question'. In carrying out his attack the cavalry commander had lost 46 officers and 329 men, and worn out the survivors and their horses, whilst expending valuable ammunition which could not easily be replaced. Major General Oranovski's 1st Independent Cavalry Brigade was also on the First Army's right flank, 50 miles to the rear; without clear orders. Nahichevanski made no effort to contact it nor ensure that Oranovski protected the XX Corps as the Cavalry Corps advanced to engage the

Landwehr. Rennenkampf reacted sharply to Nahichevanski's 'quite unsuccessful' action, singling out the 3rd Cavalry Division's commander (Lieutenant General Belgard) for special criticism. To the corps commander he declared: 'If those in command are not worthy of their appointments, you must in duty bound have no pity, otherwise all responsibility will devolve entirely on you'. The First Army commander therefore appeared not to blame Nahichevanski, but he did condemn 'your completely unsatisfactory reports. I know nothing or at any rate very little about your operation and about your losses almost nothing'.[16]

## BATTLE OF GUMBINNEN

On 19 August, ignorant of the cavalry's disappearance northwards, the Russian XX Corps commander (General Smirnov) believed that his flank was protected. Approaching the Stallupönen–Gumbinnen railway line from the north-east, he drove back German forces in his path. Then, without the First Army's cavalry corps cover or adequate reconnaissance, Smirnov's right-hand 28th Division (Lieutenant General Laskevich) was suddenly hit by the German 1st Cavalry Division with forward elements of the I Corps and pushed back with heavy loss. At 1 p.m., however, Smirnov assured Rennenkampf that the 28th Division had only been lightly attacked by dismounted cavalry. Realizing that the Germans were attempting an outflanking tactic, he therefore intended to drive northwards to frustrate them. Eventually, after more fighting, by evening both the XX Corps' divisions reached their respective objectives. The III Corps (General Yepanchin) in the Russian centre met little opposition. But, due to the hilly and forested terrain, it only reached the line Traknen–Enzuhnen, although it did establish outposts along the Rominte river. As night fell, the First Army camped on a line midway between Stallupönen and Gumbinnen stretching south-west through the Rominten Forest for almost 40 miles. Certain that the German I Corps was in full retreat, Rennenkampf did not order general, defensive preparations but left precautions to local commanders. So confident was he, that 20 August had been

**General August von Mackensen (1849–1945).** In 1869 Mackensen joined the Saxon Army, which was absorbed into that of the German Empire two years later. Commanded the German XVII Corps during the battles of Tannenberg and the Masurian Lakes. Promoted field marshal in June 1915.

designated a rest 'to bring up lines of communication organisations and the units remaining in the rear'.[17]

Prittwitz had less pleasant intentions. Having moved his HQ to Nordenburg the previous day, during the morning of 20 August Prittwitz aimed to attack along the length of the Russian line. On the German left (northern) flank, Francois' I Corps plus the 1st Cavalry Division and the Königsberg Main Reserve would move against the Russian right, Smirnov's XX Corps north of the Stallupönen–Gumbinnen railway line. As the infantry advanced north-east through the Zulkiner Forest, the cavalry rode ahead towards Pillkallen intent on exploiting the gap left by the absent Russian cavalry. On Francois' right, marching east from the Angerapp river, General von Mackensen's XVII Corps would engage the Russian III Corps. South of Darkehmen, as General von Morgen's 3rd Reserve Division moved towards Goldap on its right, the German I Reserve Corps (under the command of Lieutenant General von Below) would take on the Russian IV Corps. Now reorganized after its trauma on the previous day, the 2nd Landwehr Brigade in the far north was ordered to hold the line of the Inster river. The Battle of Gumbinnen, the second clash of the war in East Prussia, was about to commence. Refugees clogging the approach roads would, however, severely delay Mackensen and Below, leaving Francois initially to attack alone.

The Russian XX Corps was totally surprised at 3.30 a.m. when German artillery began its bombardment; four heavy and twelve field batteries to six with the Russian 28th Division. 'No individual firing could be heard; it was as though a gigantic kettle was boiling', an observer recorded.[18] With German aircraft overhead, shortly after dawn Francois' 1st and 2nd divisions emerged from the forest and field gunners moved up to fire over open sights. At 7.10 a.m. the Russian 28th Division asked for urgent artillery support; fifty minutes later the German I Corps launched a frontal attack. The Chief of Staff reported at 11 a.m. that the 28th Division 'disorganised by the extent of their [sic] casualties … began to retreat in different directions', while still resisting stoutly. When the Russians reoccupied this area 'whole companies lay in lines with their officers and with their battalion commanders, as it were frozen in the very attitude in which death had overtaken them'[19]; ten officers and 300 men of the 112th Ural Infantry Regiment were buried in a common grave at Brakupönen. During 19 and 20 August the 28th Division lost 104 officers and 6,945 other ranks, representing 60 per cent of the twelve battalions involved in the fighting. The 28th Division's withdrawal exposed the flank of the 29th Division (Lieutenant General Rozenshield-Paulin), which hastily reorganized to counter the Germans, making good use of its field artillery. By the evening of 20 August, therefore, the XX Corps had stabilized. Arguably, the 29th Division's prompt action had prevented the whole right flank of the First Army from being turned.

Meanwhile, in the centre at 6 a.m. troops of the German 35th Division of the XVII Corps attacked outposts of the Russian III Corps. The Russian 25th Division commander (Lieutenant General Bulgakov) quickly threw forward more men and, although its centre yielded, the Division's northern flank stood firm against Lieutenant General Brodrück's contingent from the Königsberg Main Reserve. The Germans were therefore sucked into a salient, whose sides were held by the Russian 25th and 27th divisions which vigorously counter-attacked. By 3 p.m. the remnants of the German 35th Division were streaming back westwards. When German artillery began seriously to damage the subsequent pursuit, at 6 p.m. a halt was called with the 25th Division on the line Lasdinehlen–Sodinehlen. The Division had incurred 35 officer and 3,145 other rank casualties during the day, but captured several hundred prisoners. A company commander in the 5th Grenadier regiment of the 35th Division (Captain K. Hesse) wrote of running into 'an invisible wall of fire …The fire of the Russian artillery was here more terrible than in any other sector, and the Russians were especially successful in developing flanking fire from their batteries'.[20] The graves of some 1,000 men from the German 35th Division bore silent witness to that.

On the III Corps' left, the Russian 27th Division had also distinguished itself, after initially coming under fire at 7 a.m. and having its outposts driven in an hour later. Using hilly terrain as cover, by 9 a.m. infantry of the German 71st Brigade of the 35th Division had advanced to approximately 1,000 yards from the Russian line, when they ran into a 'well constructed' position. Continuing to edge forward for another 300 yards, they were finally brought to a halt after suffering heavy casualties. 'It was like hell opening out before us. No enemy was to be seen, nothing but the fire of thousands of rifles, of machine guns and of artillery', Hesse recalled.[21] Determined not to be thwarted and seeking to exploit the advantage that they believed had been gained against the 25th Division during the morning, the Germans continued to bring up reinforcements to launch a fresh series of attacks between 11 a.m. and 3 p.m. After two field batteries had unwisely come into action in the open and been devastated, the Germans began to fall back at about 4 p.m. hotly pursued by Lieutenant General Adaridi's 27th Division. 'In view of the general situation', the Russian advance was stopped after a half-hour; it had captured 12 guns, 25 ammunition waggons, 20 other vehicles, 13 machine guns, 2,000 rifles and some 1,000 prisoners. During that day the Russian 27th Division suffered 21 officer and 950 other rank casualties, 12 per cent of its effective strength.

**Battle of Gumbinnen, 20 August between 3.00 and 4.00 p.m.**

| | |
|---|---|
| ▬ | Russian army unit |
| ▬ | German army unit |
| ◄ | German attack |
| ◄ | Russian attack |
| ▪▪► | German withdrawal |
| ▪▪► | Russian withdrawal |
| ▬ | German defensive lines |
| ▬ | Russian defensive lines |

Immediately south of the 27th Division, the Russian 40th Division (Lieutenant General Korotkevich) came under artillery and small arms fire near Sodehnen shortly after 9 a.m.; but here once more steadiness averted disaster. The German 36th Division continued to peck away there and around 2 p.m. two regiments of the Russian centre and left at last gave way. Only swift commitment of his reserves saved the day for Korotkevich, who was later criticized for counter-attacking without proper artillery support and thus incurring needless casualties among the 31 officers and 2,022 other ranks listed for 20 August. Nonetheless, by 3 p.m. the Germans were also in retreat in this part of the line. Rennenkampf sent the tsar a captured machine gun as a trophy of war, and news of a resounding Russian victory would cause church bells to be rung in St Petersburg.

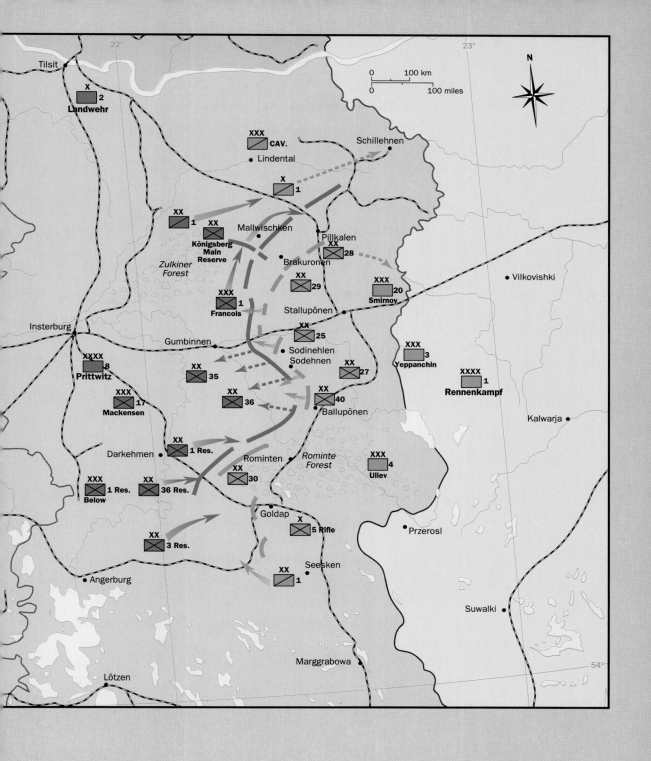

**Harvest, 1914.**
Propaganda claims
that German mili-
tary reapers were
prospering during
August 1914.

The performance of Russian cavalry that day on the northern flank of First Army would, however, cause considerable adverse comment. Encouragingly, the Russian Independent Cavalry Brigade moved up on the XX Corps' right, but then it mysteriously withdrew to its start line at Schillehnen 20 miles east – Oranovski's later excuse was that he had waited on the fringe of the battle until 5 p.m. but promised artillery support had not materialized. Moreover, he had established contact neither with Nahichevanski nor the XX Corps: 'The horses are worn out and the fighting strength of squadrons is 70–80 troopers', he claimed.[22] Meanwhile, fifteen miles away, Nahichevanski dithered; his lassitude allegedly explained, like Napoleon's at Waterloo, by a painful bout of piles. He neither went to the aid of the XX Corps nor advanced on Insterburg to threaten the German rear. On the left flank, south of the Rominte Forest, Gurko's force successfully patrolled the Seesken area; the 30th Division of the IV Corps advanced until it encountered the German I Corps along the line Kurnehmen–Wilkatschen–Wronken. No substantial confrontation took place here, as the major action occurred further north, and the German 3rd Reserve Division (ordered north from Lötzen at midday) arrived too late in the evening to affect matters that day.

Despite acknowledging the setback in the centre, the German Eighth Army staff maintained that both Russian flanks could be turned and that victory was within their grasp; Hoffmann held that the platform for 'a complete success' had been established.[23] However, disturbing reports from German reconnaissance aircraft had begun to filter through. During the afternoon one pilot had seen Russian columns advancing north along the Warsaw–Mlawa road, calculating that at the present rate of progress they could cross the frontier on 21 August. An hour later more Russian troops were spotted further west, and Prittwitz began to fear that a third Russian army might be marching on Soldau and Deutsch-Eylau to cut off his line of retreat to the Vistula. On 19 August wireless interceptions had exposed Rennenkampf's plans for the following day, but they had also shown Samsonov on the move; so the reconnaissance information was not entirely unexpected. Prittwitz had assumed, though, that the poor sandy terrain and patent lack of roads and railways would slow the Russian Second Army long enough for him to eliminate Rennenkampf. Now he was not so sure.

## GERMAN INDECISION

At approximately 6.30 p.m., Grünert (the QMG) and Hoffmann (First General Staff Officer (GSO1a)) were conversing outside Eighth Army HQ at Nordenburg when they learned of a disturbing report from Scholtz, the XX Corps commander: 'The Russian Army from Warsaw with a strength of four to five army corps had begun to cross the German frontier opposite the front Soldau–Ortelsburg'. Hoffmann reflected that 'the nerves of the C-in-C and the other chiefs are not strong enough to receive this message', suggesting that it might be suppressed until after Rennenkampf's predicted defeat. Grünert expressed surprise at such an unprofessional subterfuge and Hoffmann replied that he had been jesting. Almost immediately, Prittwitz and Waldersee emerged to confirm that Scholtz's assessment had been received and announced that they had decided to 'break off the fight and retreat behind the Vistula'.[24] It transpired that Prittwitz had made up his mind some time earlier. Worried by the signs of Russian aggression in the south, during the afternoon he telephoned Francois and Mackensen, both of whom expected to overcome Rennenkampf the following day and therefore counselled against retirement. Without knowing that Rennenkampf had suffered 223 officer and 16,862 other rank casualties on 20 August (about 20 per cent of the infantry engaged), Prittwitz revealed in his telephone conversation with Francois that lack of positive information from the XX Corps and the dread that it might soon be over-whelmed had especially influenced him. Then came Scholtz's signal and the unpalatable news that Russian troops were indeed crossing the southern frontier. His decision therefore seemed eminently sensible. Not only his own orders on appointment to the East Prussian command but Schlieffen himself had considered the possibility of falling back on the Vistula; but under much more extreme circumstances. The Eighth Army had not been overwhelmed in the field.

Grünert responded that he and Hoffmann had been discussing the situation and believed that Scholtz should be ordered to cope until Rennenkampf were finished off; they estimated in no more than three days. The southern threat could not develop seriously before then. Openly displaying strain, the Eighth Army commander angrily dismissed this interference from two junior officers and left to telephone Moltke at GHQ in Koblenz: 'The situation has completely altered. New forces have appeared in the north. The whereabouts of 1st Cavalry Division is unknown', an odd appreciation considering that no new Russian units had been identified on the German left flank and the implied threat there simply did not exist. Prittwitz continued: 'Fresh forces have appeared about Lyck [II Corps]. The Narew Army [the Russian Second, dubbed by Hoffmann the Warsaw Army] is advancing in strength against Ortelsburg and Soldau. Eighth Army is therefore going behind the Vistula'. He added gloomily that he could not guarantee holding even that line; 'it can be waded across everywhere'. 'We are to break off the battle, so successfully begun and go back. It is shameful – poor East Prussia', Hoffmann confided to his diary. He and Grünert had pressed Prittwitz to continue attacking Rennenkampf on 21 August, but 'I could not get my way'.[25]

Waldersee instructed Hoffmann to draw up detailed plans for the withdrawal. However, using compasses and referring to operational maps, the GSO1a and QMG demonstrated to Waldersee that such a retreat could not be carried out easily. At the very least, the Russian force crossing the frontier must be attacked to prevent a damaging flank attack on the retiring units; the left wing of the southern invaders was closer to the Vistula than any major German unit. The discussion widened when Prittwitz returned from speaking to Moltke. Acknowledging that the Russian Second Army did pose a severe threat in the south, on the basis of Rennenkampf's lack of enterprise since crossing the frontier Hoffmann now argued that Samsonov (potentially the greater danger to the lines of communication and Berlin) could be satisfactorily dealt with before the Russian First Army. Although Prittwitz and Waldersee had not yet regained 'command over their nerves' and still intended to recross the Vistula, they did agree to attack Samsonov's left wing. So during the evening of 20 August Hoffmann worked out the orders 'which formed the bases of the battle of Tannenberg' and were issued during the night. A cavalry division near Gumbinnen would keep watch on Rennenkampf, the I Corps from Insterburg and the 3rd Reserve Division from Angerburg leave by rail immediately for the area of Allenstein to reinforce the right wing of the XX Corps, which would itself concentrate around Hohenstein. The Main Reserve of the Königsberg garrison was to cover these departures, then proceed to the Pregel–Deime river line. The XVII and I Reserve corps would slowly disengage westwards behind Gumbinnen, ready to bolster the forward cavalry division, but in reality destined to move back to West Prussia. The I and XX corps with the 3rd Reserve Division were to attack Samsonov's left wing. If the XVII and I Reserve corps together with the 6th Landwehr Brigade did successfully disengage from Rennenkampf, Hoffmann claimed that Prittwitz aimed to reunite the whole army in the area of Osterode 'with the intention of giving battle to

**General Paul Ludwig Hans Anton von Hindenburg und Beneckendorff (1847–1934).** Recalled from retirement to lead the German Eighth Army in East Prussia, he was promoted field marshal in November 1914 and appointed Chief of the General Staff in 1916. Buried at Tannenberg.

both the Russian armies east of the Vistula'. Unfortunately, the Eighth Army commander failed to tell Moltke about his change of heart.[26]

Undetected, the German formations entrained a mere 20 miles from Rennenkampf's front line, as the Eighth Army HQ moved from Bartenstein to Mühlhausen. Meanwhile the Russians remained convinced that the Eighth Army had retired from the field in confusion. In his 23 August diary entry, Knox would record the belief at GHQ in Baranovichi that three German corps were in full retreat. Indeed so confident was he that the double envelopment would succeed, that Zhilinski allocated the II Corps to First Army to mask the Lötzen fortress. Pessimistic

**General Erich Friedrich Wilhelm Ludendorff (1965–1937).**
Served in the Chief of the General Staff's department during completion of the Schlieffen Plan. Distinguished himself during the siege of Liège in August 1914 before being appointed chief of staff to the German Eighth Army in East Prussia.

members of Rennenkampf's staff, alarmed by the casualties suffered 19–20 August, recommended retirement to regroup. Rennenkampf firmly discounted that, but he saw no urgency to push forward. His planned rest on 20 August had been rudely interrupted, therefore it would happen on 21 August.

## GERMAN CHANGE OF COMMAND

That day, at German GHQ, Moltke was digesting the contents of Prittwitz's astonishing phone call. Before the war Moltke had doubts about Prittwitz's ability, but the Kaiser would not countenance removal of a personal acquaintance. Moltke realized that retreat to the Vistula would put Berlin at risk, and he could not spare substantial reinforcement from the Western Front. Bypassing the Eighth Army HQ, Moltke spoke directly to corps commanders to find that, although the position could be classed as serious, it was by no means critical. He therefore decided to replace Prittwitz and Waldersee respectively with General Paul von Beneckendorff und von Hindenburg and Major General Erich Ludendorff. Summoned from a three-year retirement, 67-year-old Hindenburg had taken part in Bismarck's wars leading to German unification (gaining the Order of the Red Eagle and an Iron Cross), attended the German Staff College and risen to command the IV Corps before retirement at his own request in 1911. 'There was no prospect of war and, as I recognised that it was my duty to make way for younger men, I applied to be allowed to retire'. He believed in the triad of God, Fatherland and Emperor as the fundamental framework of his life; the individual must be subordinated 'to the good of the community'. Service as a staff officer in Königsberg would be a bonus, a childhood spent in West Prussia an advantage in his new post. A man of imposing physical presence, his imperturbability inspired confidence. Unlike Prittwitz, he would not be easily upset. Shortly after 3 p.m. on 22 August he tersely replied to an invitation from GHQ to command the Eighth Army: 'I am ready'. Further telegrams informed him that he would have Ludendorff as his Chief of Staff and must leave at once for East Prussia.[27]

Erich Ludendorff, aged 49 and born in Prussian-occupied Poland, complemented his new commander. Tall but thick-set, he had a brusque manner that underlined dedication and efficiency. Throughout his career he eschewed social diversions, preferring devotion to professional study. He admitted that 'my frank and soldierly way of thinking' sometimes caused offence. After attending the Staff College he held divisional and corps staff appointments, and served under Schlieffen in Berlin during the time when the latter's Plan was being developed. Ludendorff had utter self-confidence. In the early months of the war, he acted as Deputy Chief of Staff to General Karl von Bülow's Second Army, distinguishing himself at the capture of the Liège fortress, where he took over as Chief of Staff at a crucial point. Later Hindenburg reflected: 'I have often described my relations with Ludendorff as a happy marriage'. In retrospect, too, Ludendorff readily agreed that they had 'worked together like one man, in the most perfect harmony'. Like Hindenburg, his Chief of Staff had committed himself to 'a life of work for our country, the Emperor and the Army'.[28]

At 9 a.m. on 22 August, when serving with the German Second Army on the Sambre river, Ludendorff received two letters from GHQ, summoning him

to Koblenz and offering him the post of Chief of Staff to the Eighth Army in East Prussia. Moltke, the CGS, wrote: 'You have before you a new and difficult task … I know no other man in whom I have such absolute trust … The Kaiser, too, has confidence in you'. He sounded a cautious, almost pessimistic, note, though: 'You may yet be able to save the situation in the East'. Moltke urged Ludendorff to 'answer this new call'; Major General Herman von Stein (Moltke's QMG) in the second letter likewise insisted, 'you must go', adding 'your task is a difficult one, but you are equal to it'.[29] Ludendorff learned that Hindenburg was his designated army commander.

There was never any doubt that Ludendorff would accept the post, within an hour setting out by car for Koblenz. He arrived at GHQ at 6 p.m. and shortly afterwards was briefed by Moltke about events since the battle at Gumbinnen

**Battle of Tannenberg, August 1914.** General von Hindenburg (centre, with binoculars), Lieutenant Colonel Hoffman (left) and General Ludendorff (right) observing the German Eighth Army in action.

on 20 August, which 'had not resulted in any decisive [German] victory'. The CGS told Ludendorff that currently the Eighth Army between Lake Mauer and the Pregel river was in 'full retreat westwards over the river Angerapp and, to the north of the Pregel behind the river Deime, [stood] the first line of defence of the fortress of Königsberg'.[30]

Having assessed this and more detailed information, Ludendorff concluded that 'the problem' might be 'serious ... [but] was not insoluble'.[31] His appreciation of the military situation was remarkably similar to Hoffmann's, and accordingly he telegraphed orders to the Eighth Army's corps commanders. Essentially, the I Reserve and XVII corps and the Main Reserve of the Königsberg garrison were to halt their retreat; the I Corps would detrain in the region of Deutsch-Eylau, well short of Gosslershausen, to join the XX Corps east of that town. Ludendorff had thus vastly strengthened German forces in the south-west of East Prussia, remarking that 'no staff officer would miss such a chance of turning to good advantage the fact that their [Russian] two armies were separated from each other'. He also required an additional Landwehr division under Lieutenant General von der Goltz to move by train from Schleswig-Holstein to the rear of the XX Corps. Any further Landwehr and Landsturm troops that could be spared from the garrisons at Thorn, Kulm, Graudenz and Marienburg were to concentrate at Strasburg and Lautenburg, due west of Soldau. At 9 p.m., having been invested by a 'very calm' Kaiser with the *Pour le Mérite* for his achievement at Liège, Ludendorff boarded a special train for Hannover, where at 4 a.m. on 23 August Hindenburg joined him; 'it was the first time we had met'. Ludendorff outlined the current situation, and after conferring for barely thirty minutes both men retired to bed. 'We thus travelled together towards a joint future fully conscious how serious the situation was and yet with perfect confidence in our Lord God, our brave troops and, last but not least, in one another', Hindenburg wrote.[32]

The train carrying Hindenburg and Ludendorff pulled into Marienburg station at 2 p.m. on 23 August, where Hoffmann ('an intellectual and progressive officer' according to Ludendorff) and Grünert met them. 'Our reception in Marienburg was anything but cheerful. It seemed like entering another world to come into this depressing atmosphere after Liège and the rapid advance in the west'.[33] News of Hindenburg and Ludendorff's impending arrival had obliquely leaked out. During the afternoon of 22 August Hoffmann phoned the I Corps' Chief of Staff to enquire about the progress of his formation. He was met with an evasive reply, which indicated that something untoward had taken place, the nature of which the Chief of Staff would not reveal. As a puzzled Hoffmann replaced the phone, the Director-General of Railways showed him a telegram announcing the arrival of the special train. 'A few hours later', Prittwitz and Waldersee learned via another telegram that they had been replaced; 'uncommonly rough' treatment in Hoffmann's eyes. During the evening of 22 August a telegram from Ludendorff announced details of his and Hindenburg's arrival the following day. Hindenburg's reaction in Marienburg on 23 August was more philosophical and historically sensitive than Ludendorff's: 'The red walls of the proud castle of the Teutonic Knights, the greatest brick monument of Baltic-Gothic, made a truly wonderful picture in the evening light. Thoughts of a noble chivalry of the past mingled with conjecture as to the veiled future'. That evening he signalled GHQ in Koblenz that he intended 'concentration of the army for an enveloping attack in the region of the XX Corps planned for 26 August'. Hoffmann later gave the impression that on 22 August Ludendorff simply endorsed the orders issued by the Eighth Army HQ. Hoffmann was furious at reports of alleged atrocities: 'There never was such a war as this, and never will be again – waged with such bestial fury. The Russians are burning everything'; the propaganda of righteous indignation seen at the outset of most modern wars.[34]

The course of events now depended on Rennenkampf. Still convinced that he had won a decisive victory at Gumbinnen on 20 August and that the Germans were in full retreat, he did not resume his westward advance until the afternoon of 22 August. During the evening of 23 August Rennenkampf consolidated his First Army along the line Pellingken–Darkehmen with Nahichevanski's Cavalry Corps on the right flank. At this stage the bulk of the

German troops were on the line Lablauchen–Gerdauen, 14 miles from the Russians in the north, 22 miles in the south. The following day, the First Army resumed its somewhat leisurely advance, still omitting to send ahead effective patrols and therefore unaware that only a weak collection of Landwehr troops and a cavalry division lay ahead. Unlike German airmen who discovered Russian troop movements along the southern frontier, their Russian counterparts appear to have missed completely the transfer of the bulk of Eighth Army southwards to confront Samsonov. This failure of Russian aircraft to spot the German movements proved pivotal. Had he known the paucity of the opposition in front of him, Rennenkampf must surely have acted more vigorously. Late on 26 August the XX, III and IV corps were occupying the line Damerau–Gerdauen, with the II Corps at Angerburg. Contrary to more widespread opinion, in Golovine's eyes Rennenkampf, a fellow cavalryman, was not guilty of 'criminal immobility', the First Army's infantry having covered the equivalent of 45 miles in three days over most inhospitable terrain.[35]

On 26 August Zhilinski remained supremely confident. He telegraphed the First Army to press the pursuit to the Vistula while masking Königsberg with two corps. Double envelopment of the German Eighth Army remained his goal. However, further south the critical second Battle of Tannenberg was already under way.

## RUSSIAN SECOND ARMY ADVANCES

When Samsonov took personal command of the Second Army on 12 August, his II Corps was forward on the right at Augustow, just 12 miles from the border. Immediately to its left (west), the VI Corps occupied a vast 65 mile east–west position south of the Bobr river between Dolistovo and Lomja, roughly 25 miles from East Prussia. About 20 miles behind it, around Bialystok, were the III Corps and part of the XXIII Corps. The XV Corps was 40 miles further west at Zambrovo, just south of Lomja.

Samsonov therefore found his corps spread thinly, his army's cohesion and efficiency further hampered by a creaky administrative system. The whole of the Second Army had only twenty-five telephones and just two field radio stations, a mere 80 miles of cable at its disposal. After reaching Ortelsburg (18 miles inside East Prussia) the VI Corps would run out of cable and thereafter rely on mounted messengers. Wireless communications between Neidenburg north of the frontier and Ostrolenka 40 miles to the south-east in Russian territory must pass through five separate stations. One Ninth Army staff officer found a pile of telegrams in the Warsaw central post office waiting for dispatch to the Second Army HQ. On enquiry he discovered that no telegraph link had yet been established with Volkovisk, so put the messages in a bag and delivered them by hand. The XXIII Corps complained that howitzer shells must be carried in straw-lined country carts; the XIII Corps found that newly arrived recruits were seriously undertrained. Its commander Lieutenant General Klyuev pressed Samsonov for a delay: 'The lower ranks had honest Russian faces, but were only peasants in disguise whom it was necessary to train'.[1] Under orders from Zhilinski to cross the frontier quickly, the Second Army commander could not comply.

Following Zhilinski's orders of the previous day, on 14 August Samsonov issued his own to the Second Army subordinate commanders, encouraging them that reinforcements were imminent. 'The units of our I Corps ... have reached Warsaw. Units of the Guard Corps are arriving'; reference to the corps withdrawn from the First Army, which with the 1st Rifle Brigade of XXIII Corps were in limbo at Warsaw, 75 miles south-west of Zambrovo. Samsonov went on to require that by 6 p.m. on 17 August his corps should be in position from east to west: II (Augustow); VI (Lomja); XIII (Ostrolenka); XV (Rozan); the XXIII Corps' 2nd Division (Novo Georgievsk, between Warsaw and Mlawa), with the 3rd Guard Division still out of the line at Bialystok. These dispositions would allow the Second Army to penetrate East Prussia west of the Masurian Lakes, but left a significant gap between the VI and II corps. The 6th and 15th cavalry divisions under Lieutenant General Lyubomirov (the 15th Division's commander) at Tsyekhanov, would protect the Army's left flank. Two days later, 16 August, Samsonov circulated more detailed orders, without prior reference to the North-West Front commander, absorbing the two corps at Warsaw: 'Second Army, reinforced by the Guard and I corps, will attack the front Lötzen–Rudczanny–Ortelsburg–Passenheim ... executing the main turning movement round the west of the Masurian Lakes, the object being to defeat the enemy operating in the area behind the Lakes, and cut him off from the Vistula'. The II Corps would 'safeguard the right flank of the army from sallies by the enemy, who may debouch from the passages of the Masurian Lakes area', as it advanced towards its first objective, 15–40 miles inside German territory. The second objective, the line Seeburg–Rastenburg, lay a further 30 miles north and west of the Masurian Lakes. There the Second Army would meet an equally victorious First Army to complete the encirclement and annihilation of the enemy. The only recent movement detected among the German forces involved a division from the XX Corps moving to Johannisburg, and a division of the XVII Corps moving closer to Mlawa. The defences of Neidenburg, near the border, had also been strengthened.[2]

Samsonov noted that the Second Army HQ would relocate at Ostrolenka on 18 August. He went on to lay down a programme requiring the I Corps on the left to reach Mlawa, close to the frontier, by the evening of 20 August, the 2nd Division of XXIII Corps to be behind it 25 miles north of Novo Georgievsk. The Guard Corps would remain in reserve at Novo Georgievsk, 45 miles south of Mlawa. The three central corps, from right to left, the VI, XIII and XV, were ordered to reach the intermediate positions Dobylas–Grabovsk–Makov (18 August); Pupovizna–Blendovo–Prasnysz (19 August); and the start line for the invasion Domrowo–Chorzele–Zabolk by the evening of 20 August. Aware that his formations could not advance together simultaneously, Samsonov gave more specific orders to his cavalry. He required the 4th Cavalry Division (less the 4th Uhlan Regiment) to cover the gap between the II and VI corps, the 6th Cavalry Division the left flank of XV Corps and 15th Cavalry Division westwards beyond the I Corps. He did not, however, detail any cavalry to scout into German territory in accordance with Zhilinski's intentions, on 18 August.

On learning of the Second Army commander's orders, during the evening of 16 August Zhilinski reacted by telegraph. He stressed that the I Corps was controlled by North-West Front, and that the 2nd Division of XXIII Corps should replace it in the line. After further representations from Samsonov,

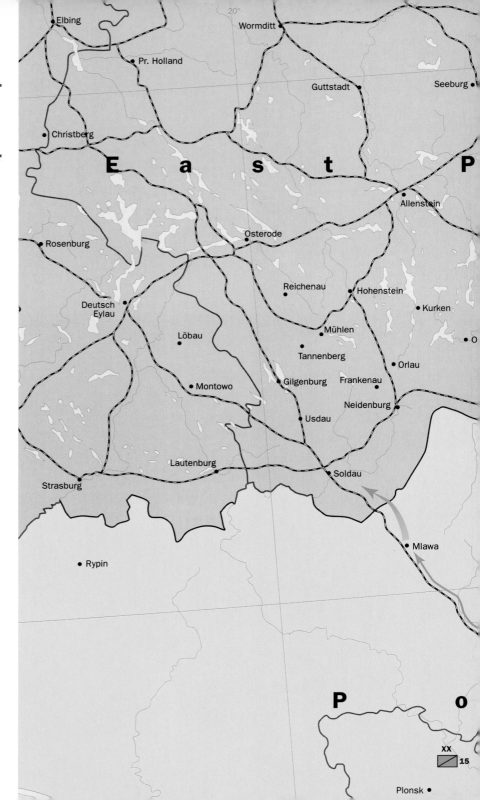

**Russian Second
Army Plan**

Russian planned movement

Russian lines of planned
advance

other army concentration
area

Elbing

Wormditt

Pr. Holland

Guttstadt

Seeburg

Christberg

E    a    s    t         P

Allenstein

Rosenburg

Osterode

Reichenau

Hohenstein

Kurken

Deutsch
Eylau

Mühlen

Löbau

Tannenberg

Orlau

O

Montowo

Gilgenburg

Frankenau

Neidenburg

Usdau

Lautenburg

Soldau

Strasburg

Mlawa

Rypin

P         O

XX

15

Plonsk

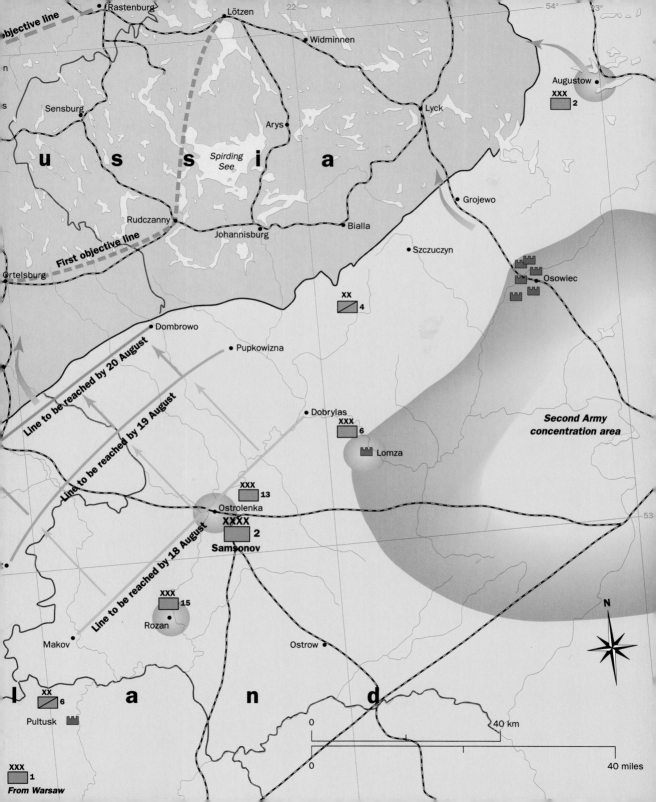

though, three days later Zhilinski did agree to transfer the I Corps to him, but not the Guard Corps. Believing that Rennenkampf was making rapid progress north of the Masurian Lakes, on 19 August Zhilinski became agitated about his Second Army's slow progress and hectored it to speed up, complaining that it was putting the First Army at risk by not advancing more quickly. Somewhat disingenuously, Samsonov replied: 'The army has been advancing without pause since the receipt of your orders, travelling daily more than 20 versts [13 miles] of sands, and consequently further acceleration is impossible'. An eyewitness recalled that 'the reservists unused to marching were exhausted and the Corps disorganised'.[3] Lack of transport animals and deficiencies in rations did not help. On one occasion horses were observed hauling half a wagon train for a mile then being unhitched to bring up the other half, before repeating the process. The XIII Corps completed nine forced marches without receiving bread.

On 20 August Samsonov circulated current situation reports. 'More than a division' of Germans had been identified in the Neidenburg/Soldau/ Gilgenburg region; advanced units in Mlawa. 'About a division' was in the Johannisburg area; 'on the Chorzele front – weak units'. The Russian First Army had fought 'a successful engagement' near Stallupönen and was 'continuing to advance to the Insterburg–Angerburg front'; his own II Corps had already crossed the frontier to occupy Lyck on 19 August. He then issued orders for 21 August. The Guard Corps, under his command from the previous day, would move to the Plonsk area as additional protection for the Second Army's left flank. General Besovrasov's corps did not subsequently cross into East Prussia and it joined the Ninth Army with the South-West Front at the end of August. Samsonov went on to order the 15th Cavalry Division to reconnoitre westwards beyond the 6th Cavalry Division to the line Serpets/Strasburg/Bischofswerder.

In the wake of the II Corps' success, the invasion of East Prussia by the rest of the Second Army was much more disjointed than Samsonov had planned. The VI Corps crossed the frontier late on 20 August, the XIII Corps the following day. By the evening of 21 August they were respectively close to Ortelsburg and Willenburg. However, the XV Corps, I Corps and 2nd Division of XXIII Corps were then still south of the border. For those inside East Prussia the signs appeared very encouraging; thus far, no significant resistance. A reconnaissance aircraft reported German columns north-west of Mlawa heading away from the frontier towards the interior; cavalry patrols reported that villages with barbed wire and trench defences had been abandoned. Samsonov, therefore, believed that the Germans were in retreat, and drew up plans for 22 August accordingly. The VI Corps was to capture Ortelsburg (10 miles into Germany), the XV Corps and I Corps respectively Neidenburg and Soldau, just over the frontier. The XIII Corps should be prepared to support either the VI or XV corps, the 2nd Division of XXIII Corps advance to Mlawa to reinforce the I Corps on the left flank. Essentially this was an exercise in consolidation, which Zhilinski saw as a woeful lack of aggression: 'I demand immediate and resolute operations', he signalled. Samsonov responded by reiterating the parlous state of his supplies. A staff officer elaborated: 'The infantry and artillery are miserably provided for. I don't know how the troops stand for it any longer. It is vital to organise a proper requisitioning system'. Klyuev, the XIII commander, concurred: 'Little comes through and then only by chance; cattle and a few poultry are the only local resources, as villages are deserted and the hay and oats uncut'.[4] On 22 August the II Corps formally transferred to the First Army, though some reports appear to place it under North-West Front not the Second Army from 13 August.

Absence of significant opposition on the ground did not mean that the advancing troops went undetected or undisturbed. General Martos, commander of the Russian XV Corps, reported continuous reconnaissance by German aircraft, one of which dropped a single bomb to the discomfort of a neighbouring flock of geese. Artillery shells and small arms fire failed to hit or deter the aerial observers; attempts by Russian aeroplanes to shoot down the German aeroplanes or airships were equally useless. 'Our aviation could not fight them. I forbade aimless infantry fire at aeroplanes, as it only produced

**Ravages of War:**
a Prussian building
reduced to rubble
during the East
Prussian campaign,
its occupants
salvaging the
remains of their
belongings.

disorder. The fire which was occasionally opened by field artillery was also unavailing, and so the enemy aviation observed us with impunity', Martos recorded. Gurko, the cavalry commander, reinforced Martos, noting that few Russians had even seen an aircraft before the German Taubes appeared over-head: 'immediately an aeroplane hove into view the men would rush for their rifles and blaze aimlessly' to the peril of Russian as well as German machines. Crossing the frontier, the XV Corps found that the Germans had destroyed Yanou and were harassing the approach to Neidenburg with isolated armed groups. Martos complained that the Cossack cavalry attached to his corps provided useless reconnaissance reports. From a distance, Red Cross flags could be seen fluttering from buildings in Neidenburg – a ruse aimed at buying time for German troops to escape by train. Cavalry in advance of the main

body identified barricaded streets and were fired on as they edged forward. So Martos ordered his artillery to bombard the town, especially the railway station, 'reducing most of the houses in the central square to ruins', according to Knox. When in captivity later, Martos would be accused of causing wilful damage and unnecessary civilian casualties.[5]

Thus, by the evening of 22 August, the VI Corps held Ortelsburg, the XIII Corps was north of Willenburg, the XV and I corps respectively in Neidenburg and Soldau. So far, so good. On 23 August Samsonov decided to straighten his line. The VI Corps would remain at Ortelsburg; the XIII on its left advance to Jedwabno and Omulefoten; the XV Corps go north-west to Seelesen. The I Corps was to stay at Soldau with the 2nd Division of XXIII Corps moving up on its right to fill the gap with the XV Corps. It was all unambitious, with

**German refugees** crowding into a park at Allenstein, having fled before advancing Russians, to receive assistance from the civic authorities (foreground).

swift progress towards the second objective of Seeburg–Rastenburg remote. In fact, Second Army now extended almost 60 miles, its dispersed corps open to piecemeal destruction. Zhilinski was right to express grave concern. He might have profited from sending a staff officer to confront Samsonov, and considering more seriously Samsonov's report during the evening of 22 August. 'The country is devastated. The horses have long been without oats. There is no bread. Transport from Ostrolenka is impossible'.[6]

## CLASH OF ARMS

At 5 p.m. on 23 August Martos' XV Corps finally encountered strong opposition, when it ran into a defended position between Orlau and Frankenau. German machine gunners took a heavy toll of infantrymen who unwisely raised their heads as they crawled across open potato fields. Although the 31st Regiment occupied Lahna after fierce fighting at 8.30 p.m., by nightfall the Russians were still 700 yards short of the main German line. During the darkness Russian troops crept closer and at dawn on 24 August launched a furious bayonet charge. That morning Orlau fell to the 1st Brigade of the 8th Division, Frankenau to the 2nd Brigade of the 6th Division, both final assaults being strongly supported by field artillery and howitzers. The Russians were too exhausted, though, to pursue the Germans, having suffered heavy loss; three regimental commanders, fifty officers and 2,500 men killed or wounded. One regiment lost nine out of sixteen company commanders; one company 120 out of 190 men killed. The British military attaché later quoted estimates of 4,000 Russian and 6,000 German casualties. Surveying the scene, he concluded that 'the Russians used the spade freely … I saw rifle trenches scooped out within 130 yards of the defenders' trenches'.[7]

Samsonov wrongly concluded that the Germans aimed to defend Deutsch-Eylau, Lautenburg and the vicinity of the lakes at Hohenstein. He therefore asked Zhilinski to approve a change of objective to the line Allenstein–Osterode. He argued that this would allow him to deal with the German troops assumed (wrongly) to have been driven back by Rennenkampf.

The Mlawa–Soldau railway line would bring up supplies for his attack and Allenstein–Soldau would be a better springboard for an advance into the German heartland. Samsonov seems to have assumed that encirclement of the Eighth Army west of the Masurian Lakes was no longer necessary. Zhilinski agreed that the Germans were in flight towards the Vistula, and accepted the need to vary the original objective of Seeburg–Rastenburg. But he was more cautious than Samsonov. Noting that 'the enemy has apparently left only insignificant forces facing you', he required the Second Army commander to secure his left flank with one corps at Soldau, then to 'execute a most energetic offensive against Sensburg–Allenstein', which must be carried out by 25 August. 'The object of your manoeuvre is to attack and intercept the enemy retiring before General Rennenkampf and to cut off his retreat to the Vistula'.[8] Zhilinski and Samsonov believed that no German forces were in a position to assault Samsonov's left flank as the Second Army pressed north. A grave mistake.

With Zhilinski's support, therefore, at 5.30 p.m. on 23 August (ironically at about the same time that the XV Corps ran into entrenched German positions between Orlau and Frankenau) Samsonov issued orders for the next two days. The Second Army must 'energetically' attack northwards to reach the line Pilben–Waplitz on 24 August; Sorquitten–Bischofsburg–Wartenburg–Allenstein–Hohenstein the following day. On 24 August the I Corps from the Soldau area would 'cover the operation in the Deutsch-Eylau direction'. The 4th Cavalry Division, reaching Sensburg (theoretically 30 miles from Rennenkampf) on 24 August, would reconnoitre the sector bounded on the right by Rastenburg–Allenburg, the left Rössell–Domnan, paying special attention to Lötzen. The 6th and 15th cavalry divisions, after reaching Locken on 24 August, would operate towards Heilsburg–Tsinten 'cutting the enemy's lines of retreat to the Vistula, demolishing railways and bridges and destroying L. of C. [lines of communication] organisations' – a truly herculean task. Ominously, in line with his pessimistic report to Zhilinski, Samsonov anticipated that his supply train would not cope with the planned advances:

'During the execution of these operations, troops are to be supplied for the most part from local resources' – that is, live off the land. At 7.30 p.m. on 23 August Samsonov issued a thoroughly misleading directive to his Army. 'The enemy, defeated by our First Army, is hastily retreating from the line of the River Angerapp covered, apparently, on the left flank of our army by units of the XX Corps in the Allenstein area'.[9] For almost three hours German troops had been resisting the XV Corps in the Orlau/Frankenau area. They were in strength some 23 miles south of Allenstein, and an airman attached to the Russian I Corps had reported two divisional encampments near Gilgenburg.

However, bolstered by the XV Corps' capture of Orlau on 24 August, Samsonov once more pressed Zhilinski for permission to adjust his objective to the line Allenstein–Osterode, convinced that the Germans were retreating in that direction. Aware that Rennenkampf had lost contact with the major German units and believing that the Eighth Army was falling back on Königsberg, Zhilinski reluctantly agreed. However, the North-West Front commander insisted that the VI Corps and the 4th Cavalry Division should cover the gap between the Lakes and Allenstein. This would create a danger-ously dispersed Second Army, justifiable only if the Germans were indeed in confused flight. The VI Corps would be separated from Samsonov's main force of three and a half corps by 30 miles, effectively two to three days' march away. The Second Army would now be spread thinly over 75 miles arching north-east to south-west, hampered by the need to pass wireless messages via a cumbersome communications system. Some units did not receive Samsonov's orders of 23 August until two days later, when they should have completed their movements.

Knox drove from Mlawa to the Second Army's HQ in Ostrolenka early on Monday 24 August. Just before lunch Martos signalled Samsonov that the XV Corps had captured two artillery pieces and two machine guns and intended to camp that night north of Neidenburg at Orlau and Frankenau. Major General Postovski, the Second Army's Chief of Staff, complained 'of the diffi-culty of assuming the offensive in a region which had been purposely left roadless in order to delay the expected German offensive'. With insufficient time to organize efficient transport lines (each corps being responsible for its own arrangements), he sardonically dubbed the entire invasion 'an adventure'.[10] Significantly, Samsonov's intention of moving his HQ to Ortelsburg, a railway junction 10 miles inside East Prussia, was delayed by failure as yet to establish a telegraph link between there and Zhilinski.

The following day, 25 August, Knox travelled on to the XV Corps HQ at Neidenburg, where Martos emphasized that his patrols had been fired on by civilians during the afternoon of 22 August, though inhabitants insisted that only German troops had been involved. As the British military attaché went on towards Lahna he noted outbursts of firing aimed 'at a German aeroplane which floated above us at about 1,000 metres, quite unharmed'. At Frankenau Lieutenant General Torklus, commanding the 6th Division, underlined the deadly accuracy of German machine guns and estimated that three divisions of the German XX Corps had faced him during the past few days. On examining the ground and evidence of the fighting, Knox thought only one German division could have been involved. He acknowledged, though, that communication with the North-West Front and the adjacent XIII Corps had broken down and that the XV Corps had been allocated too wide an area to cover. In his diary Knox mused that 'dear old Torklus seemed more interested in the psychology of his men and in the effect on them of their baptism of fire than in any preparations for a continuation of the advance'. Alarmingly, on 25 August Knox recorded reports that 'the enemy is preparing to offer battle on the line Mühlen–Nadrau–Lansk'. Fortunately, he did not know that Russian orders for the advance on 26 August had been intercepted by German wireless operators, and that the German I Reserve Corps was already close to the VI Corps on the Russian right.[11]

By the evening of 25 August the Second Army had its right flank at Sensburg (the 4th Cavalry Division, east of the Masurian Lakes), left flank at Zielun (the 15th Cavalry Division). The VI Corps was at Bischofsburg, the XIII at Kurken, the XV Corps at Orlau and Frankenau, the 2nd Division of the XXIII Corps at

Lippau and the I Corps around Usdau and Koslau with the 6th and 15th cavalry divisions on its left. That day, however, Samsonov received disturbing news. He learned of a strong German force at Gross Gardienen and another approaching Lautenburg from Strasburg, on the extreme left flank of the Second Army. Cavalry on the Army's right flank near Sensburg reported German troops passing through Rastenburg moving west on 24 August, which Samsonov decided posed no major problem. Postovski signalled Zhilinski for permission to halt, emphasizing that since 17 August the troops had marched an average of 20 miles a day in the face of the enemy. Moreover, in view of his current knowledge of German dispositions, Samsonov wanted to wheel left. The North-West Front HQ proved unsympathetic, once more complaining 'that the Second Army's offensive has progressed more slowly than he [Zhilinski] expected'. The enemy had left Insterburg on 23 August and, therefore, was at least two marches away – use of railways and the evidence of fighting south of Allenstein did not apparently impress the staff at North-West Front HQ. Zhilinski would not sanction a pause until the line Allenstein–Osterode had been reached; any westward variation was positively forbidden. To Samsonov's QMG, Major General Filimonov, who had been dispatched to explain in person the impending threat to Second Army's left and rear, Zhilinski insultingly replied: 'To see an enemy where he does not exist is cowardice, but I will not permit General Samsonov to play the coward, and demand of him the continuation of the offensive'.

Samsonov therefore had no option but to issue orders for 26 August, requiring the XIII and XV corps to continue their advance to Kellaren–Schonfelde–Hohenstein–Reuchenau–Gilgenburg. The VI Corps would remain as cover at Bischofsburg. Attaching the 1st Rifle Brigade and the 3rd Guard Division of XXIII Corps (both now in the line) and the 6th and 15th Cavalry divisions to I Corps, he ordered its commander General Artamonov to act aggressively against any threat to his left flank and the

**Front-line German troops firing rifles and a machine gun at a Russian aeroplane.** So much ammunition was wasted in futile exercises like this that commanders on both sides forbade their troops to fire at any aircraft.

**German Rumpler-Taube aeroplane in action.** This artist's impression is unrealistic for few aerial dog-fights took place in East Prussia. Although Hindenburg complained that aerial reconnaissance reports were often vague, German airmen were more effective in identifying troop movements than Russian.

Russian lines of communication, even in the face of superior numbers. The entire success of the Second Army's thrust northwards depended on the I Corps, Samsonov reminded Artamonov; a vast oversimplification of the developing scenario, as it turned out.[12]

## BATTLE JOINED

The German deployments had been swift, more organized and stronger than Samsonov or Zhilinski suspected. Hindenburg believed that the Russians had 800,000 men and 1,700 guns in the field to Eighth Army's 210,000 and 600 respectively. Therefore, 'we had not merely to win a victory over Samsonov. We had to annihilate him. Only then could we get a free hand to deal with the second army, Rennenkampf'.[13] Since fragmented wireless interceptions and aerial observations on 20 August had revealed the Russian Second Army on the move along the southern frontier, the danger of Samsonov either linking with Rennenkampf or attacking German lines of communication with the Vistula and western Prussia had been a particular concern. It prompted Prittwitz's panic decision to withdraw and the subsequent, amended plan to deal with Samsonov before finishing off Rennenkampf. On 22 August intelligence officers estimated that there were some 30 miles between the Russian First Army and the retiring German corps with no noticeable attempt to follow them. In the south, five Russian army corps and three cavalry divisions were advancing towards the line Soldau–Ortelsburg. With these details in mind and assisted by discovery of Zhilinski's 13 August directive in the wallet of a dead Russian officer, the German movement orders finalized on 23 August (though set in motion by Hoffmann on 21 August) went ahead. By 25 August, on the German left around Hohenstein, the XX Corps covered forest openings vulnerable to Russian penetration. After entraining during the evening of 21 August but having its journey subsequently truncated by Ludendorff, the I Corps had arrived in the vicinity of Deutsch-Eylau and Gilgenburg, poised to support the XX Corps on its right, the 3rd Reserve Division covering the I Corps' left after marching 33 miles. On the Russian right (German left), the

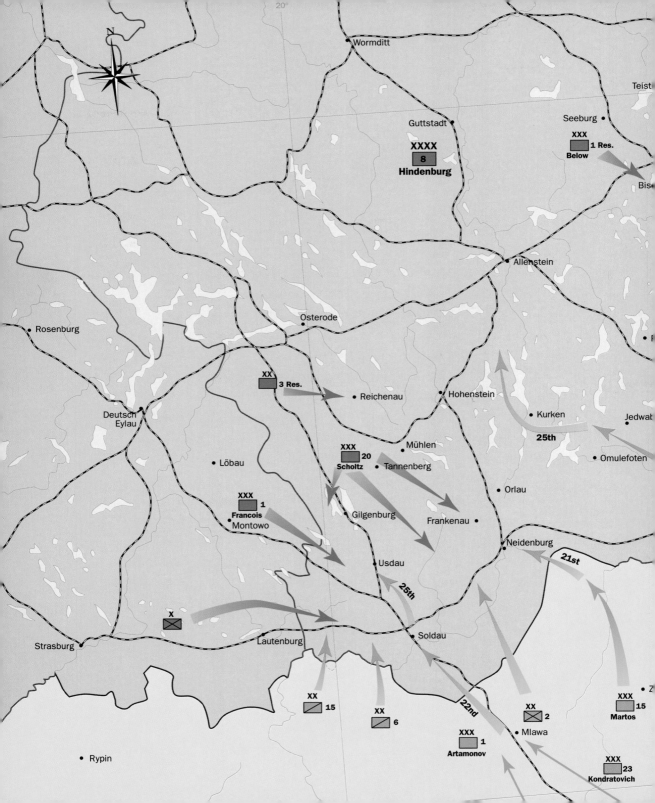

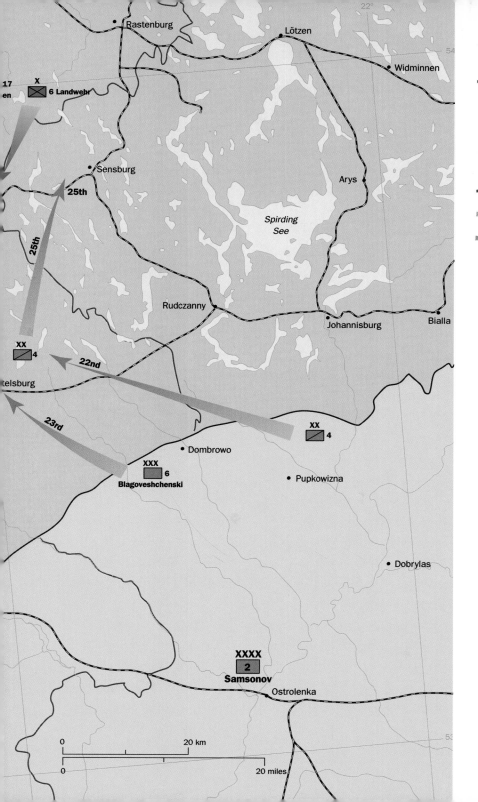

**Russian Second Army,
21–25 August,
and German Plan,
26 August**

→ Russian attack with dates

→ German counter-attack
26–27 August

Rastenburg

Lötzen

Widminnen

17
en

X
6 Landwehr

Sensburg

Arys

25th

Spirding
See

25th

Rudczanny

Johannisburg

Bialla

XX
4

22nd

telsburg

23rd

XX
4

Dombrowo

XXX
6
Blagoveshchenski

Pupkowizna

Dobrylas

XXXX
2
Samsonov

Ostrolenka

0                    20 km

0                    20 miles

XVII and I Reserve corps had also marched much of the way south, the former 100 miles in five days. Lieutenant General Baron von der Goltz's Landwehr division from Schleswig-Holstein was not expected at Biessellen until 28 August, after a 550 mile train journey.

During the afternoon of 23 August and early the following day, the 37th Infantry Division on the left of Scholtz (XX Corps commander) was strongly attacked but drove off the Russians with heavy losses. Scholtz then withdrew the Division, prompting the Russians to believe that a general retreat had started and Samsonov to order a hot pursuit. On 24 August, as the German Eighth Army HQ moved to Riesenburg, Hindenburg and Ludendorff drove south to see Scholtz and his Chief of Staff (Colonel Hell) at Tannenberg, close to 'a simple monument there [which] bore silent witness to the deeds and deaths of [Teutonic] heroes'.[14] Scholtz told them that his clash with Russian forces in the Orlau/Frankenau area on 24 August had been serious, but he now intended to withdraw the 37th Division to Gilgenburg/Mühlen. This would make the Russians march further in an attempt to outflank him and gain time for Francois to bring the I Corps into action on 26 August. The Eighth Army commander and his Chief of Staff agreed, with the proviso that the 3rd Reserve Division remained west of Hohenstein. Hoffmann would later write of 24 August, 'from the point of view of the High Command that evening was the most difficult of the whole battle'. Ludendorff revealed that the Eighth Army received an unexpected bonus that day, when an intercepted Russian wireless message 'gave a clear idea of our opponents' dispositions for the next few days'. It appeared that Samsonov's I Corps on the Russian left advancing towards Soldau 'should echelon sharply to the left and undertake the covering against Thorn', while the VI Corps on the right would move forward along the line Ortelsburg–Mensguth towards Lötzen.[15]

Another insecure Russian transmission on 25 August confirmed that Rennenkampf would offer no threat in the immediate future. However, Ludendorff believed that the Russian Second Army would be in a position to attack Scholtz's XX corps on 26 August. He therefore visited Francois near

Montowo on 25 August, ordering him to attack Usdau at 5 a.m. on 26 August in co-operation with Scholtz's right wing. Francois' protests that a frontal attack would prove costly and that his artillery lacked ammunition were brusquely dismissed. As Ludendorff left the I Corps HQ he received yet more transcripts of Russian wireless communications, this time involving Samsonov's detailed orders. At 8.20 p.m. on 25 August Hindenburg issued the orders, which the next day would initiate the Battle of Tannenberg. Additional troops of the Russian I Corps had been 'reliably ascertained' entrenched in the Bergling–Grieben area opposite the German XX Corps. Despite this complication, Scholtz's corps must not only hold its own position but 'co-operate in the I Corps offensive by an attack by its right flank in the direction of Grieben–Jankowitz'. The XX Corps 'must be ready to attack on the whole front, in strength on the right wing'. The German I Corps would, with its right flank, occupy the heights of Seeben at 4 a.m. and no later than 10 a.m. launch an assault from there southwards towards Usdau. Lieutenant General Von Mülmann's Landwehr force would remain under Francois for these operations; the 3rd Reserve Division be prepared to march on Hohenstein. Until 7 a.m. on 26 August, the Eighth Army HQ would be at Riesenburg, then move to the southern outskirts of Löbau.

Rennenkampf's inactivity remained crucial to German success. After the 1st Brigade of the 1st Cavalry Division had been ordered to Sensburg, from 27 August only two cavalry brigades would face the Russian First Army north of Lake Mauer. Despite the Russian commander's turpitude, Ludendorff recorded that Eighth Army's position was 'nonetheless one of tremendous gravity'; Hindenburg wondered whether the Russians had abandoned their two-pronged attack in favour of an assault on Königsberg. Nevertheless, the I and XX corps would attack Samsonov's left flank, the XVII and I Reserve corps his right. Basically, Ludendorff envisaged the German I Corps breaking through towards Neidenburg to act in conjunction with the I Reserve and XVII corps to surround the bulk of the Russian Second Army. 'We had to confine ourselves to this plan, if we wished to succeed', Ludendorff noted. He resisted the temptation to drive south of Soldau over the frontier to deal with the Russian I Corps, which 'would have been absolutely annihilating, but the forces at my disposal were insufficient'. The Chief of Staff of the Eighth Army later recalled that 'Rennenkampf's formidable host hung like a thundercloud to the north-east … He need only have closed with us and we should have been beaten'.[16]

Hindenburg wrote that 'this day [25 August] marked the conclusion of the stage of expectation and preparation'.[17] Zhilinski's dream of encircling the German Eighth Army was about to be ruined by a pre-emptive double envelopment of his own Second Army. Samsonov would pay for his lack of reconnaissance and for allowing the VI Corps to be isolated. Oblivious to the impending German threat, on 26 August he intended his central XIII and XV corps to press forward respectively on Allenstein and Osterode. The VI Corps was to stand firm at Bischofsburg, while detaching one of its divisions towards Allenstein in support of the XIII Corps, as the I Corps took steps to counter the perceived threat in the west from Lautenburg.

**Tannenberg,
26 August**

→  Russian attack

- - ▶  Russian withdrawal

➤  German counter-attack

## 26 AUGUST

As 26 August dawned, 'the first day of the murderous combat which raged from Lautenburg to north of Bischofsburg' over a 60 mile front,[18] the Russian I Corps occupied high ground around Usdau, Meischlitz and Ruttowitz, with forward elements at Seeben and Grallau. Under Artamonov's command, the 6th and 15th Cavalry divisions protected the left flank, giving the Russians a 50:9 squadron advantage in this area. Yet the main German formation remained undetected, only Mülmann's 5th Landwehr Brigade at Lautenburg being identified. The Russians appeared obsessed with earlier reports of troops advancing from that direction and did not envisage a serious threat from the north. Their defensive position on the dominating ground was good though, with clear fields of fire. Nevertheless, there was an important 7 mile gap between the I Corps' right flank and the 2nd Division of XXIII Corps on the

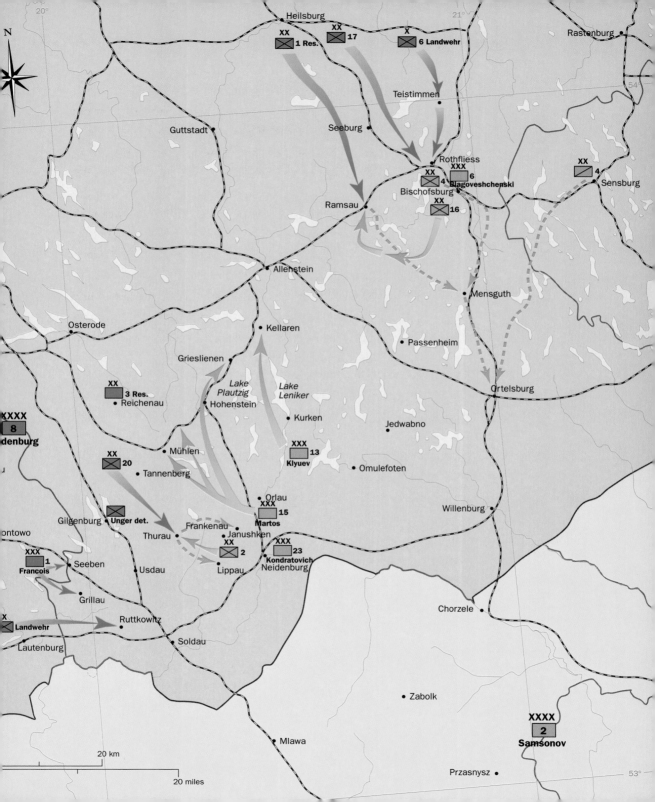

XV Corps' left. Artamonov compounded this weakness by withdrawing a brigade from his right to attack Lautenburg. The absence of effective Russian aerial reconnaissance was again marked.

Opposing the Russian I Corps, aware that lack of artillery at Gumbinnen had cruelly exposed advancing infantry to devastating fire, an obstinate Francois failed to launch the planned dawn assault, pleading yet once more lack of field artillery. Nonetheless, he had his leading division in position before the Seeben Heights by 8 a.m. To the amazement of the Eighth Army HQ, which unaccountably believed that the Heights were under attack at 7.30, Francois requested flexibility to be allowed to fix the timing of his own assaults. He was firmly told by Ludendorff twice that morning not to delay beyond noon. So by 1 p.m. the Seeben Heights had fallen, just as the Russian I Corps' attack on Lautenburg was repulsed. Lieutenant General von Conta, commanding the 1st Division of the victorious German I Corps, argued that his troops were too exhausted to attack Usdau that day, and Francois agreed. Later Ludendorff would accept that at this stage Francois 'quite rightly' refused to move forward until his whole corps and its associated supply columns had concentrated, 'the condition of the railways in East Prussia being far from good'. Almost certainly, he meant that the vastly increased traffic had stretched the carrying capacity of the network. He added, though, that German plans were disrupted because of exhaustion and losses through 'continual fighting', indirectly supporting Conta. Hence the German I Corps rested during that night short of the town preparatory to carrying out Francois' orders on 27 August: an artillery bombardment at 4 a.m. followed by the main attack an hour later. It emerged later that the Eighth Army HQ had ordered the I Corps 'to take up its position at 4 a.m. and intervene with the greatest energy'; thus the initiative had not actually been Francois'.[19]

On Artamonov's right the 2nd Division of the Russian XXIII Corps had force-marched to cover the XV Corps' left and be in a position to reach the main Hohenstein–Reichenau road on the evening of 26 August. Early progress seemed encouraging, until its troops came under heavy fire after capturing

Thurgau and a German counter-attack scattered them between Lippau and Neidenburg; the 7th Regiment losing 75 per cent of its strength. Critically, the Gilgenburg–Neidenburg road now lay unprotected. As the 2nd Division retreated in confusion, north of it the XV Corps advanced, capturing Hohenstein before being held up south of Mühlen by the 41st Division of the German XX Corps. Martos discovered that the Germans were along the Drewenz river in a forested area between him and his objective, Osterode. He therefore deployed during the night of 26–27 August to prepare for a dawn attack. To the XV Corps' right, the XIII Corps had enjoyed a successful day on 26 August, despite setting off late (until 1 p.m. Klyuev confidently expected cancellation of the order to continue advancing north), clearing lakes Lansker and Plautzig en route for Allenstein. At dusk, Klyuev signalled Samsonov for

**Russian dead.**
Heavy casualties were incurred during the battle of Tannenberg near Hohenstein, west of the Masurian Lakes. The dead infantry are from the Russian XV Corps.

permission to assist Martos' XV Corps which he knew had come under fire.

The Second Army commander, however, showed only a vague awareness of the day's events by ordering the VI Corps (by then in retreat) to leave a screen at Bischofsburg and join the two corps to its left. The XIII and XV corps were ordered to close on Allenstein and Osterode, the I Corps to protect the Russian left flank. When no reply arrived to his request to help Martos, Klyuev unsuccessfully tried to reach General Blagoveshchenski (VI Corps), unaware that heavy traffic between Zhilinski's HQ and Novo Georgievsk was swamping weaker stations. Following Samsonov's orders during the evening of 26 August, he wished to jeopardize neither his own attack on Allenstein nor the VI Corps' projected advance on the town from Bischofsburg. He did not raise Samsonov and the eventual contact with the VI Corps at dawn on 27 August proved indecipherable. To add to his worries Klyuev's men were desperately short of food, having been without bread and biscuits for some days. Capture of Allenstein would alleviate the pangs of hunger.

In his diary on 26 August, Knox commented on the 'bad staff work' of the Russians, highlighting the inability of a transport colonel to read a map. A column of staff cars therefore went 3 miles down the wrong road before having laboriously to turn round on a sandy track; 'It did not occur to him that he should have reconnoitred the road in his light car, while the transport cars were taking in petrol at Neidenburg'. The British military attaché reflected that 'the Russians seem to muddle through in a happy-go-lucky way', with no sense of urgency. He also described encountering casualties being taken to the rear: 'One of the men had had an extraordinary escape, a bullet entering on the right of his nose and traversing the head, going out behind the left ear'. Sitting up in the cart, the man 'confessed he did not feel quite well!'[20]

On the Russian right, ordered to remain on the defensive, the VI Corps anticipated little action on 26 August. The 16th Division occupied Bischofsburg, the 4th Division being in position just north at Rothfliess with outposts thrown forward from Allmoyen to Teistimmen. The 4th Division had only a few Cossacks for reconnaissance purposes, but showed complete lack of initiative in not using them: commenting later on the German advance from the north, Colonel Servinovich (the Chief of Staff) said that 'no orders for reconnaissance in this direction had been received'.[21] When the 4th Division commander (Lieutenant General Komarov) did learn during the night of 25–26 August that Germans were in Lautern and Seeburg, he rashly assumed that these comprised a screen for troops retreating from Rastenburg and even more rashly determined to attack Lautern, 10 miles north of him. Meanwhile, obeying Samsonov's order of the previous day, Blagoveshchenski instructed the 16th Division to go to Allenstein on the morning of 26 August. It had made scant headway, when at noon the VI Corps commander ordered it back to Bischofsburg. Just 4 miles from there, Blagoveshchenski amended his order. One regiment with artillery support would continue eastwards, the rest of the division move north towards Seeburg to assist the 4th Division, which had come under strong attack from the German 36th Infantry Division and 6th Landwehr Brigade.

Mackensen's German XVII Corps had acted positively in accordance with orders. Deploying east of Lake Lautern on 25 August, at dawn the following day following an artillery bombardment it attacked the Russian 4th Division at Rothfliess. As it did so, on its right the I Reserve Corps and the 6th Landwehr Brigade made for Ramsau, aiming to turn the Russian VI Corps' left flank. The Russian troops at Rothfliess, though heavily outnumbered, resisted stoutly until their commander eventually ordered them back to Bischofsburg at 6 p.m. By then, seventy-three officers and 5,283 men, two batteries of artillery (sixteen guns) and eighteen machine guns had been lost. The withdrawal was by no means orderly. Units in Bischofsburg were also in retreat, and the bulk of the 16th Division had been checked at Ramsau by the German I Reserve Corps after marching 19 miles since noon. By the evening of 26 August the Russian VI Corps was in disorganized retreat towards Ortelsburg and Mensguth. The right flanks of the XIII and XV corps were thus exposed, without their commanders, Samsonov or Zhilinski knowing. No message from the VI Corps reached any of them. Thus the North-West Front commander, ignorant of the Second Army's deteriorating situation, ordered Rennenkampf to dispatch two corps to invest Königsberg, while the remainder of his First Army pursued 'those enemy troops which do not take refuge in Königsberg' towards the Vistula. Reading this order, Rennenkampf was entitled to assume that an attack on the German fortress constituted his primary task, and that the bulk of the enemy supposedly routed at Gumbinnen had withdrawn within its defensive perimeter. He therefore issued instructions which commenced, 'Königsberg will be closely blockaded', followed by an order to force the Deime river in the first instance. Further south, despite lacking any news from the VI Corps, and encouraged by other optimistic reports, Samsonov believed that his plans were going well.[22]

The Germans had more doubts. During the evening of 26 August considerable concern was expressed at the Eighth Army HQ in Löbau. Wireless interceptions had revealed that Rennenkampf's II Corps (recently acquired from the Second Army) was moving through Angerburg, intent on meeting Samsonov's right flank. Hindenburg, noting that 'the crisis of the battle now approached', admitted misgivings about concentrating on Samsonov; perhaps he should have contained the Second Army and finished off Rennenkampf. Ludendorff, 'doubtful whether the enemy would give us time to carry out our plans', feared that Russian cavalry patrols would disrupt his left flank. Refugees packing the roads were also severely hampering military columns. Hindenburg recorded that, nonetheless, 'we overcame the inward crisis, adhered to our original intention and turned in full strength to effect its realisation by attack'.[23] Having made their decision and about to retire to bed, Hindenburg and Ludendorff received a telephone call from Lieutenant Colonel Tappen, Chief of Operations at GHQ in Koblenz. Within the next week, Moltke intended to dispatch three infantry corps (two were actually sent) and a cavalry division to the Eastern Front and sought advice as to where they should go. Ludendorff replied unenthusiastically that they would arrive too late for the present battle.

During the afternoon of 26 August Samsonov drove from his HQ at Ostrolenka to Neidenburg, held by the XV Corps, arriving shortly before 5 p.m. There he dined with Brigadier General Knox, whom Samsonov whimsically noted was unarmed despite being in enemy territory. This prompted Postovski (the Second Army Chief of Staff), according to Knox 'generally nervous and goes by the name of "the Mad Mullah"', to fetch a sword for the British officer, who remarked that Samsonov appeared 'content and satisfied'.[24] During the meal a staff officer entered to say that Artamonov, the I Corps commander, insisted on talking to Samsonov as a matter of urgency. It emerged that in Usdau Artamonov expected to be attacked by two or three divisions from the north-west (Francois' German I Corps troops on the Seeben Heights) and by another from Lautenburg. No battle was then in progress, though. Samsonov agreed that part of a brigade of the 3rd Guard Division at Soldau should be put under Artamonov and, not realizing that it had already fallen back, sent word for the 2nd Division of the XXIII Corps to cover the I Corps' right flank.

Thus at the close of 26 August, unknown to Samsonov, on his right the German XVII and I Reserve corps, supported by the 6th Landwehr Brigade advancing from Lötzen, had driven the VI Corps from Bischofsburg in disarray. The right flank of the XIII Corps, which had not yet met stiff opposition, had thus been exposed; the XV Corps after heavy fighting was nonetheless preparing to attack the left flank of the German XX Corps. With the defeat of the 2nd Division of the XXIII Corps, the right flank of the Russian I Corps was in grave danger as it awaited an onslaught from Francois' German I Corps.

## 27 AUGUST

Aware of the crucial nature of this phase of the battle, Hindenburg and Ludendorff were in position on a small hill 4 miles south of Gilgenburg to witness the opening of the I Corps' bombardment of Usdau with twenty-eight field and eight heavy artillery batteries as ordered at 4 a.m. Ludendorff revealed that their journey was not simply to observe the bombardment, but primarily to oversee co-ordination of the I and XX corps. With Mülmann's 5th

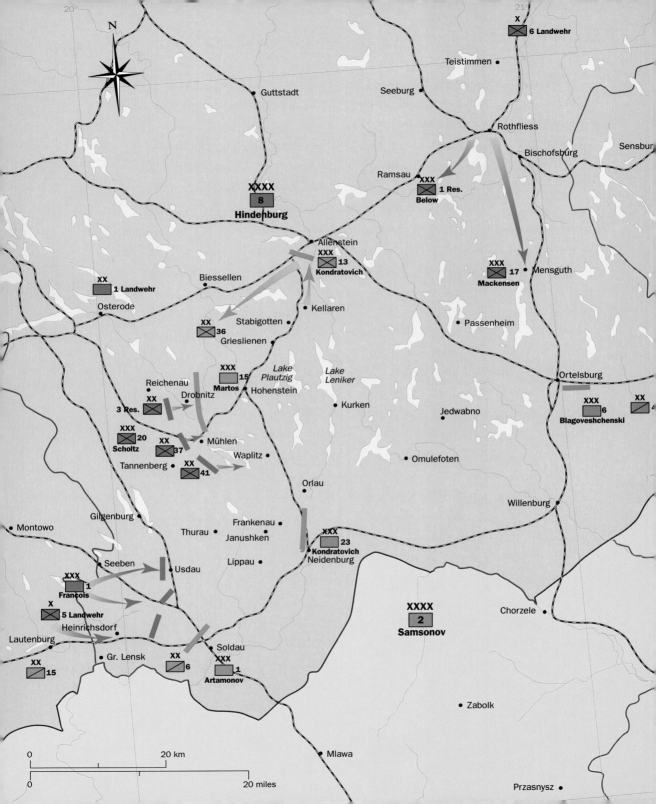

Landwehr Brigade reinforced by troops from the Vistula fortresses protecting his right flank, Francois sought to attack Usdau from north-west and west. A detachment of the I Corps led by Lieutenant General von Schmettau (Thorn Main Reserve commander) would advance south from Bergling simultaneously to hit Artamonov's right flank through the gap left by the retreating 2nd Division of the Russian XXIII Corps. The senior Eighth Army officers were not disappointed. By 10 a.m. the Russians had been ejected from their forward positions, their telegraph, telephone and wireless communications so disrupted that Samsonov could not be informed of these unpleasant developments. By 11 a.m. the Germans were in Usdau; Samsonov's left flank had effectively been turned.

**Tannenberg,
27 August**

→ Russian attack

▬ Russian line

→ German counter-attack

▬ German line

Suddenly, however, Francois learned that, reinforced by the 1st Rifle Brigade of the XXIII Corps, on his right Russian troops had counter-attacked to take Heinrichsdorf, as their 15th Cavalry Division at Zielun threatened to disrupt his lines of communication. The German I Corps commander therefore halted his advance, while a detached division dealt with this new development. Realizing that they were effectively exposed by the defeat of the Russian I Corps at Usdau and now themselves under attack, the Russians soon abandoned Heinrichsdorf. Artamonov's corps had now been broken. By nightfall, Lieutenant General Sirelius commanding the 3rd Guard Division of XXIII Corps had rallied a mixed bag of five regiments from different divisions and six batteries of artillery astride the railway north of Soldau. But Francois had taken a giant step towards eliminating the Russian left flank and advancing the right arm of the encirclement of Samsonov's Second Army. Knox, the British military attaché, left Neidenburg for Mlawa at 1 p.m. that day as shells began to fall, noting universal alarm and occasional shouts that 'the German cavalry was upon us'. He noted, too, a depressing visit that day to a hospital established in a former German school. There was 'very little sign of forethought and organisation. No beds had been collected. The wounded were lying every-

**Russian wounded.**
Russian field
hospitals were
set up in captured
Prussian buildings
such as schools.
In one of these,
a priest blesses
wounded lying on
straw in cramped
conditions.

where, on the straw or on the floor. Many with the sun streaming in on their heads'.[25]

On the German I Corps' left, the XX Corps advanced more slowly than expected and Ludendorff therefore signalled Francois urgently to detach a division to Rontzken, north of Neidenburg, against the Russian XV Corps' left flank. Concerned at developments, Hindenburg and Ludendorff reached Scholtz's HQ at noon. They learned that the corps commander, anticipating an attack on his left, had placed the German 3rd Reserve Division and Major General Fritz von Unger's Graudenz garrison troops in defensive positions along the Drewenz river. Initially the right and centre encountered scant opposition. However, fearing a Russian attack in the vicinity of Mühlen, Scholtz sent the 37th and 41st divisions south of Lake Mühlen to hit the

Russian rear at Waplitz. A report that the Russians had indeed broken through at Mühlen caused Scholtz to divert the 37th Division there, while the 41st Division went on alone to Waplitz. As it emerged that the Mühlen information had been false, news arrived at HQ of an attack in the Drewenz sector. Goltz's Landwehr division from Schleswig-Holstein had arrived in the area of Osterode and Biessellen, but could not reach the battlefield in time. There were no other reserves, so the exhausted 37th Division was ordered there, though it would not arrive until the following day. Meanwhile, the 41st Division had stopped short of Waplitz. The German XX Corps had not enjoyed a very successful day.

Back in Mlawa on 27 August, information filtered through to Knox that Samsonov had moved the left flank of the XV Corps from Hohenstein to Mühlen, thus altering the axis of attack, while the XIII and VI corps closed on Allenstein. This appeared to open an unhealthy gap between the XV and the other corps. 'I can only hope he has not under-estimated the strength of the German advance from the west and north-west', Knox prophetically wrote. A French pilot, Poiret, serving with the Russians, estimated that the Germans had three corps in action, and that they aimed to contain the Russian centre and right while pushing back the left to cut lines of communication with Mlawa and Warsaw. Knox observed that the German force was generally imagined to comprise the XX, XVII and a reserve corps, but admitted that hard intelligence was sparse. That evening the Russian I Corps transport began retreating through Mlawa with tales of 'dreadful' and 'awful' experiences, and it emerged that Artamonov's troops had been ejected from Usdau. In the east, German units were in Passenheim.[26]

Early in the day's exchanges Martos had informed the Second Army Chief of Staff (Postovski) that he intended to wheel left to meet a German corps (Scholtz's XX) advancing on his flank. He pressed for Klyuev's XIII Corps to abandon its movement towards Allenstein and join him. Postovski agreed to put one brigade from the XIII Corps under Martos. Unfortunately, ordered to outflank the Germans at Drobnitz, the brigade lost its way in thick forest and, during the afternoon, returned to Hohenstein in some confusion. Elsewhere fierce fighting had occurred around Drobnitz and Mühlen; the Germans were still holding the Drewenz line. At about 5 p.m. Postovski phoned Martos with orders from Samsonov that the following day the XV, XIII and VI corps were to concentrate against Allenstein. Martos vigorously disagreed with such a drastic change of direction. He argued that he was heavily engaged along his whole front and that the Germans were being strongly reinforced. Moreover, a reconnaissance pilot had identified significant German troop movements east of Drewenz. When Postovski insisted, Martos offered his resignation, but heard no more.

On Martos' right the XIII Corps had pressed on towards Allenstein as ordered. Having encountered no significant opposition, early on 27 August Klyuev prepared to answer Martos' personal plea for assistance by diverting a division to Hohenstein and another to Stabigotten, whence it could support either the XV or the VI Corps. Then came the order from Samsonov to detach a brigade to help the XV Corps, so Klyuev abandoned his more elaborate arrangements. The rest of the corps duly occupied Allenstein at 4 p.m., with some of the troops overexcited because they thought themselves in Berlin. More critically the Russians failed to secure the railway as they looted supplies and food, allowing a German armoured train to bombard the 1st Division's camp south-west of the town. Klyuev's own elation was soon dented, too. One Russian pilot landing at Allenstein reported heavy fighting between Martos and the Germans; another spoke of two columns marching on Wartenburg from the south-east, which Klyuev assumed was the Second Army's VI Corps. He therefore gave this pilot a message for Blagoveshchenski, with details of his current dispositions. Klyuev's orders were duly carried out by the Russian pilot, but the columns had been German and therefore he landed behind enemy lines. So the German I Reserve Corps commander secured invaluable information at no cost. Still believing that the troops seen close to Wartenburg were friendly, Klyuev sent a mounted reconnaissance party to contact them. Their divisional commander was not unduly worried when they were fired on,

as this often happened to Russian scouts from their own cautious infantry.

The day closed in a state of considerable disorganization for the Russians in the centre. Late in the evening Martos heard via a divisional commander that Samsonov had put the XIII Corps under his command for a combined attack on the Germans facing him. Klyuev had protested that he could not be in position for such an attack until 29 August and additionally requested a XV Corps staff officer to brief him about Martos' deployment.

On the German left (Russian right) during 27 August, the XVII and I Reserve corps had continued to pursue the disrupted Russian VI Corps, leaving a rear-guard at Lautern should the Russian II Corps, last seen at Angerburg, turn south. Convinced that the greater threat involved the Russian XIII and XV corps, Hindenburg diverted both German corps south-west until he heard that

**Abandoned position.** German artillery often surprised Russian units in the open. This field battery has been devastated before it could withdraw its ammunition limbers. Note the dead horses.

Blagoveshchenski had rallied the remnant of his corps near Ortelsburg and the Russian XIII Corps was fast closing on Allenstein. So Below's I Reserve Corps was sent south of Wartenburg, preparatory to moving on Allenstein or Ortelsburg. These were the columns erroneously believed by Klyuev to be Russian. The German XVII Corps would go to Mensguth with a detachment blocking the Passenheim Gap. By midnight all these tasks had been accomplished.

During the afternoon of 27 August, thinking that his I Corps had repulsed the Germans and that the 2nd Division XXIII Corps was at Frankenau, the XV at Mühlen and the XIII at Allenstein (the last being the only correct assumption), Samsonov dispatched his orders for 28 August. The I and XXIII corps were to maintain their positions at all costs; the XV and XIII under Martos at dawn to attack towards Gilgenburg to threaten the flank and rear of Germans in front of the I and XXIII corps; the VI Corps to go to Passenheim. At 11.30 p.m. he reported to Zhilinski that the Second Army now faced the German I, XVII, XX and I Reserve corps. On the left, Artamonov had withdrawn to Soldau in the afternoon 'without sufficient reason',[27] and been sacked by Samsonov in favour of his 22nd Division's commander, Lieutenant General Dushkevich. The Second Army commander admitted that the 2nd Division of the XXIII had been driven back, but it was now reorganizing at Neidenburg. Mühlen, he wrongly claimed, was in Russian hands with the Germans retreating south-westwards; the VI Corps north of Mensguth, apparently in good order.

Ludendorff's orders issued during the evening of 27 August were straightforward: 'The reinforced XX Corps, von der Goltz's Landwehr Division, I Reserve Corps, and XVII Corps will envelop the Russian XIII and XV corps'[28]

## 28 AUGUST

In Hindenburg's words, 'the bloody struggle continued to rage on 28 August'. At 7.15 a.m. Samsonov sent a decisive telegram to Zhilinski. The Second Army commander no longer intended to stay at his Army's HQ. Noting that the 'badly disorganised' I Corps had been withdrawn to Ilowo, leaving only a rearguard at Soldau, he continued: 'I am going immediately to the Headquarters of the XV Corps at Nadrau to take over personal control of the advancing Corps. I am closing this office and will be temporarily out of communication with you'.[29] In retrospect Knox thought this a courageous decision, but practically it was a tacit admission that Samsonov would no longer provide overall leadership. Taking charge of one corps' operation displayed a level of personal frustration; it had no strategic relevance. Before leaving Neidenburg, still unaware of the disaster at Bischofsburg, Samsonov sent a signal to Blagoveshchenski ordering him to commit the 4th Cavalry Division to the battle, to hold Ortelsburg and the Passenheim Gap. It underlined how hopelessly out of touch he was.

The day had already started ominously for Knox, when he witnessed a Zeppelin attack on Mlawa railway station, which killed six and wounded fourteen. 'One was filled with impotent rage against the machine, and it was with genuine delight that I heard it had been brought down and its crew captured', he wrote, demonstrating current fury at indiscriminate aerial bombing of civilians.[30] Shortly after this early morning incident Knox drove back to Neidenburg, arriving at 8.15 a.m. He observed that German shelling and burning villages seemed much closer to the road than when he drove in the opposite direction the day before. Learning that Samsonov had already left, Knox set off with a staff officer and a Cossack escort for Jedwabno only to come across the army commander poring over maps with his staff by the roadside. When the conference concluded, Samsonov ordered eight of the Cossack escort to hand over their horses to him and his staff. Knox was about to mount another, when Samsonov spoke to him quietly. 'He said that he considered it his duty to tell me that the position was very critical. His place and duty was with the army, but he advised me to return while there was time, as my duty was to send in "valuable" reports to my Government'. He went on to explain that the I Corps, 2nd Division of the XXIII Corps and the XV Corps had all been forced back and that he had only just heard (at 9 a.m.) of VI Corps' rout on the right at about 6 p.m. the previous afternoon (27 August); a defeat correctly claimed in German records for the evening of 26 August. Nor had Mühlen fallen to the Russians as reported on 27 August. Samsonov believed that the Neidenburg–Mlawa road (along which Knox had so recently driven) was no longer safe, so all transport was being re-routed to Ostrolenka via Willenburg. He confided to Knox that he was unsure of the outcome of this battle, but was certain that it would not affect the ultimate result of the war. Before he and his seven staff officers rode off north-westwards, Samsonov mused hopefully: 'The enemy has luck one day, we will have luck another'.[31] On the Second Army's right flank, during 28 August Blagoveshchenski had rallied the remnants of the VI Corps around Ortelsburg, with the 4th Cavalry Division patrolling on his left. But he did not receive Samsonov's order to move on Passenheim until after 1 p.m., and decided that his infantry were too exhausted to do so that day.

**Tannenberg, 28 August**

→ Russian attack

▬ Russian army position

- - ➤ Russian withdrawal

➤ German counter-attack

▬ German army position

Also unaware of the VI Corps' fate as 28 August dawned, Klyuev prepared to withdraw his XIII Corps from Allenstein towards Hohenstein in support of the XV Corps and in accordance with orders transmitted through Martos the previous day. He dispatched all unnecessary transport to Kurken by the shortest route, leaving a battalion behind to organize its departure. Before Klyuev could come to its aid, the battalion was surrounded and overwhelmed by German troops assisted by armed citizens firing from vantage points including the houses. Even worse news followed. Approaching Grieslienen, Klyuev's vanguard learned that German cavalry had cut communications with the XV Corps, as machine gun fire from the rear of the XIII Corps' column announced a hot pursuit by German units which had occupied Allenstein. The rearguard, the 143rd Dorogobujski Regiment, fought such a prolonged, bitter action that it lost almost 500 men including its commander. But it held off the pursuers and the main body of the XIII Corps remained intact. Then a Cossack brought the depressing information that the transport column and its escort had been captured or wiped out. During the

N

20° 21° 54°

• Teistimmen

• Guttstadt • Seeburg • Rothfliess

**XXX**
**1 Res.**
Below

• Bischofsburg • Sensburg

**XXXX**
**8**
**Hindenburg**

• Ramsau

**XXX**
**17**
Mackensen

• Allenstein

**XXX**
**13**
Klyuev

• Mensguth

• Biessellen

• Kellaren

• Passenheim

• Osterode

• Stabigotten

**XXX**
**15**
Martos

• Grieslienen

**XXX**
**1 Landwehr**

*Lake Plautzig*

*Lake Leniker*

• Ortelsburg

**XX**
**4**

**XX**
**37**

• Reichenau

• Hohenstein

• Kurken

**XXX**
**6**
Blagoveshchenski

**XXX**
**20**
Scholtz

• Drobnitz

• Jedwabno

**XX**
**3 Res.**

• Mühlen

• Waplitz

**XX**
**41**

• Tannenberg

• Omulefoten

• Orlau

**XXXX**
**2**
**Samsonov**

• Gilgenburg

• Lahna

• Frankenau

**XXX**
**23**
Kondratovich

• Grunfliess

• Willenburg

• Thurau

• Rontzken

• Muschaken

• Seeben

• Sallusken

• Neidenburg

• Usdau

• Lippau

**XXX**
**1**
Francois

• Heinrichsdorf

• Chorzele

**XX**
**6**

• Gr. Lensk

• Soldau

**XX**
**5**

• Zabolk

20 km

**XXX**
**1**
Dushkevich

• Mlawa

20 miles

• Przasnysz

53°

afternoon and early evening Klyuev launched repeated assaults on Hohenstein, without success. As darkness fell, the XIII Corps remained pinned in surrounding woods. Realizing that it was trapped between lakes in the south and increasing numbers of German troops in the north and on his flanks, Klyuev decided to rest that night and attempt to break through to the XV Corps at first light.

At midnight on 28 August a mounted messenger brought orders from the Second Army HQ for the XIII Corps to retreat during the night via the gap between lakes Plautzig and Lansker to the Kurken area, where it would receive further orders; the XV Corps was already retiring to Neidenburg. Klyuev knew that the chosen passage between the lakes had been covered by the Germans, so opted for the Schwederich defile.

Meanwhile, during the early hours of 28 August, in darkness the left flank of the XX Corps came under small arms fire from its left, and at dawn the Germans launched a strong attack. Using his reserve regiment Martos success-fully counter-attacked near Waplitz capturing eighteen officers and 1,000 men, whom he sent to the rear under Cossack escort. As this column made its way south, in mid-morning after leaving Knox, Samsonov and his staff appeared on the hill above Mühlen from which Martos was directing opera-tions. On being informed about the prisoners, the Second Army told a surprised Martos: 'You alone can save us', which the commander of the XV Corps remarked 'struck me unfavourably'.[32] Aware that Artamonov had been defeated, Martos assumed that strong, fresh reinforcements were in the line near Frankenau. Samsonov corrected this impression; only weak forces were there resisting the German advance on Neidenburg. Martos immediately counselled withdrawal of his corps, lest it be cut off. Postovski argued for a delay pending the arrival of the XIII Corps. So the XV Corps remained near Hohenstein, while its commander, Samsonov and his staff anxiously scanned the north-eastern approaches for Klyuev. In vain. At 3 p.m. German shells scat-tered a XIII Corps regiment attached to Martos in the north, and its panic spread to the transport lines.

Still Samsonov hesitated. As darkness fell, with no sign nor communication from XIII Corps Martos suggested falling back on Chorzele, but Samsonov incorrectly said that this was occupied by Germans. The Second Army staff now drew up orders for the XIII and XV corps to concentrate at Neidenburg. Samsonov told Martos that, once he had issued orders to his subordinate commanders, he should ride as quickly as possible to the town and take charge of its defence. Almost simultaneously shells began to rain on the hill and rear areas. Leaving Martos to organize the withdrawal, Samsonov and his small entourage rode off. Over an hour later Martos and his escort caught up with them, resting by the roadside. Samsonov impressed on Martos the seriousness of the situation, but maintained that if Neidenburg could be held all was not lost. His delusion underscored yet once more the critical lack of information about German movements and the appalling state of Russian communications.

During 28 August General Kondratovich dug in west of Frankenau, 10 miles south of Martos, with a weak collection of XXIII Corps units. Initially he did well, beating off attacks in the morning and capturing 1,000 prisoners from the German XX Corps. But when another heavier assault came during the afternoon, Kondratovich panicked, dashed about aimlessly and at length donned a German coat to escape through enemy lines west of Neidenburg with his driver. He would be dismissed for abandoning his command and replaced by the 3rd Guard Division's commander, Sirelius.

Early that day Lieutenant General Dushkevich (Artamonov's replacement) had withdrawn the bulk of the I Corps along the road to Mlawa, leaving a rearguard in Soldau. Attacked at 5 a.m., that rearguard resisted for five hours before being overrun. Its relative success in the face of vastly superior numbers suggests that the Russian I Corps ought to have counter-attacked the advancing Germans in strength. A massive breakdown in morale among staff officers, as well as unit commanders, alone can explain this omission. Once more demonstrating his complete lack of understanding of the strategic situation, during the evening of 28 August Samsonov ordered the I Corps to attack German forces approaching Neidenburg.

**Destruction.**
Soldau, close to
the southern border
of East Prussia,
witnessed heavy
fighting and artillery
bombardment
during the battle of
Tannenberg. The
extent of damage
to its buildings is
well illustrated.

In their advanced HQ at Frögenau close to Scholtz's German XX Corps, at 7 a.m. on 28 August Hindenburg and Ludendorff heard artillery and small arms fire as the attack launched against the Russian XV Corps three hours earlier progressed. Their overall plan that morning was for the XX Corps to engage the Russian centre from west and north. Lieutenant General von Below's I Reserve Corps would drive south of Allenstein to hit its rear and also send a detachment to secure the Schwederich defile (due to concerns about Allenstein the force was not actually dispatched). Francois' German I Corps and Mackensen's XVII Corps were respectively to harass the Russians at Soldau and Ortelsburg. Learning that a Russian division still held Allenstein, Ludendorff told Below and Mackensen to prevent this linking with the Russian II Corps at Rastenburg to threaten German lines of communication.

Scholtz ordered his troops to attack along a line from south of Mühlen to north of Hohenstein, with Lieutenant General Baron von der Goltz's 1st Landwehr Division (weakened by non-arrival of five battalions and three batteries due to the railway delays deplored by Ludendorff) advancing at 5 a.m. against the Russian right flank from Osterode. In the south the 41st Division of the XX Corps would attempt to turn the Russian left flank at Paulsgut. This was the force, exhausted after a lengthy night march, success-fully counter-attacked by the Russian XXIII Corps reinforcements and driven back towards Wronowo. However, further north, in the centre of Scholtz's attack Lieutenant General von Morgen's 3rd Reserve Division redressed the balance, moving forward at 8.30 a.m. without waiting for news from the south. Scholtz only learned of this movement when it was under way, and wisely ordered the 37th Division to support Morgen; while Goltz's Landwehr troops closed on Hohenstein from the north-west. As a result Hohenstein and Morken were taken, the Russian XX Corps seriously compromised. By night-fall on 28 August the Germans held a line from west of Waplitz and Nadrau to Hohenstein.

However, with defeat of the 41st Division causing a check on the XX Corps' progress, the major impetus rested with the I Corps, whose commander

(Francois) continued to plough an independent furrow with panache. He had ordered his 1st Division, Mülmann's 5th Landwehr Brigade and Schmettau's force to attack the Russian I Corps at Soldau and once that fell to make for Neidenburg with Mülmann acting as rearguard. Meanwhile, another force comprising the 2nd Division, cavalry and artillery would go straight to Neidenburg. Soldau duly fell and shortly after 10 a.m. its conquerors led by Francois set off for Neidenburg. At 11 a.m. a messenger from Ludendorff arrived with a change of orders timed 9.10 a.m. In view of the 41st Division's repulse, 'the I Corps must immediately send the [2nd] division ...to Rontzken to avert ... a breakthrough on the part of the enemy. Schmettau's detachment will attack at once in the same direction ... Haste is essential'. Francois did not respond, and went on towards Neidenburg. A second message arrived at 1 p.m., timed 12.25: 'The I Corps is to assist the 41st Infantry Division, which is apparently retreating on Wronowo. The Corps is also to continue the general pursuit in the direction of Lahna.' A strange element of pleading then appeared: 'The I Corps will render the greatest possible service to the Army by operating in accordance with these instructions.'[33] This time Francois compromised: the 2nd Division would go to Lahna, the remainder of the Corps continue to make for Neidenburg.

The reason for Ludendorff's apparent indecision was lack of firm evidence of the troops' progress, because he was served by 'a very ineffectual field-telephone', which connected him to Scholtz but no other formation commander. As reports came in piecemeal from staff officers, obliged to make physical contact with subordinate headquarters, 'our first impressions were by no means favourable'. Dreading a Russian assault on the right wing of the XX Corps coupled with the recurring nightmare that Rennenkampf might yet advance, Ludendorff referred to the possibility of 'a grave crisis' developing.[34]

Temporarily, his fear seemed real. A mile short of Neidenburg Francois was attacked from the north by the revitalized Russian XXIII Corps' 2nd Division. The attackers, however, were quickly driven off towards Salusken and Rontzken. Arriving east of Neidenburg during the evening, Schmettau's force

**Restoring normality.** Ortelsburg, in the path of the Russian VI Corps during the battle of Tannenberg, suffered heavy damage. After the Russians had been driven off, the market place began to function again among the ruins.

set off to capture Muschaken in the early hours of 29 August. Meanwhile the 1st Division of the I Corps consolidated on the outskirts of Neidenburg. Lieutenant Heeder of the 33rd Regiment later described how during the advance on Neidenburg several shot-down aircraft had been passed, which may go some way to explaining the paucity of Russian intelligence information in the area.

The situation further east, on the German left flank, was less satisfactory. The I Reserve and XVII corps made little contribution to the assault against the Russian XV and XIII corps and failed to annihilate the VI Corps around Ortelsburg. To some extent lack of information reaching the Eighth Army HQ further complicated matters. As a result, during the morning a change of plan was announced with both corps now ordered to march on Allenstein. Instead of the whole XVII Corps, Mackensen was to send only a detachment against Blagoveshchenski. Unhappy that he was now required to abandon a close pursuit and turn much of his corps north-westwards, nevertheless Mackensen obeyed. He therefore trailed Below, as a small mixed force of infantry, cavalry and artillery pursued the Russian VI Corps. Unedifying exchanges between Mackensen (the senior commander) and Below over road priority further slowed progress. Meanwhile Below had been ordered to advance his main force on Grieslienen, as Allenstein was only held by a few Russians. The administrative dispute with Mackensen ensured that the I Reserve Corps could not take Grieslienen that day.

Reports of clashes with Russian cavalry 25 miles north-east of Allenstein during the afternoon caused further German dismay until lack of supporting Russian infantry was confirmed. However, thereafter a protective cavalry screen was maintained in that area and important road and railway crossings south of the Russian First Army put under guard. That day, too, another change of plan delivered in person by Ludendorff over the phone had sent the German XVII Corps south again, parallel to the Bischofsburg–Ortelsburg road, to Jedwabno. By nightfall on 28 August Mackensen had occupied Passenheim.

As he did so, the Eighth Army HQ moved to Osterode, Hindenburg staying at the inn where he had been during manoeuvres in 1881. That afternoon, he and Ludendorff left by car from Frögenau for Mühlen to encounter a rabble of fleeing transport drivers, yelling that the Russians were on their heels. Ludendorff told staff officers to draw their pistols and bar the road. This restored order, and it emerged that the drivers had mistaken a column of Russian prisoners for an enemy advance. However, the chaos persuaded Hindenburg to abandon his journey. That evening, although the full facts were unknown to him, the strategic position was a good deal more encouraging for the Germans. After the war Ludendorff would reflect that the battle had now been won; at the time he could not be so sure. Three Russian corps (VI, XV, XIII) were being driven south-east towards the frontier and threatened with encirclement between the German XX, I Reserve and XVII corps,

**Into battle.** German infantry advancing during
he East Prussian campaign. Note the distinctive
Pickelhaube helmet and heavy packs.

as the German I Corps drove its Russian counterpart towards Mlawa in the west. Yet Ludendorff fretted about reports that Rennenkampf was at length on the move. Samsonov must be finished off quickly.

## 29 AUGUST

Ludendorff's orders for 29 August, issued from Frögenau at 5.30 p.m. the previous day, required the I and XX Corps to press the pursuit, Landwehr and garrison troops to pause and reorganize, Below's I Reserve Corps to consolidate at Allenstein. No instructions were issued to Mackensen and the XVII Corps, whose position at that time was unknown (he had not then reached Passenheim). Francois' specific orders to the I Corps required Schmettau to take Willenburg, the 1st Division to move to Muschaken, having secured Neidenburg, and the 2nd Division to occupy Grunfliess so cutting off the Russian southern escape route. Ludendorff recorded that he aimed to execute a classical Cannae double envelopment with the jaws clamping shut at Willenburg.

The exhausted and to some extent disorientated Russians – Klyuev allegedly had not slept properly for ten nights – were meanwhile attempting to stabilize the situation, not altogether clear as to whether they were preparing for a counter-attack or a fighting withdrawal. Pausing only briefly at Orlau after leaving Martos, Samsonov and his staff rode on during the night of 28–29 August to Yanou, where the Second Army's rear HQ had been established after crossing the frontier. There Samsonov issued his last orders. The XIII Corps would retire to Chorzele, the XV and XXIII corps to Yanou, the latter two covering the XIII by taking up position in the area of Lahna, Samsonov being unaware that it was in German hands. Samsonov was clearly ignorant of his XIII Corps' parlous state, for he ordered it to force-march to Muschaken by dawn 30 August, ready to move on Neidenburg. Finally, the Second Army commander appeared to abdicate all executive responsibility: 'The general control of operations for the retreat of the three corps has been delegated by the Army Commander to the senior Corps Commander'.[35]

Moving through the night, the XIII approached the Schwederich Gap. The leading troops passed through German-held Morken without challenge until a machine gun opened up from a house near its eastern end and other positions joined in from surrounding heights. Under heavy fire, therefore, the Russians crossed a dam 14ft wide. As dawn broke, the back of the column managed to skirt the danger area. An artillery rearguard protected the main column and a gallant cavalry charge led by Colonel Kaknovski held off German infantry attacks. Once clear of Morken the XIII Corps still had to negotiate the Schwederich Gap, but the opposition there proved curiously mute. Reaching Kurken at noon, Klyuev discovered that he had been given command of the three corps.

On Klyuev's left the XV Corps, the partial XXIII Corps and the 6th Cavalry Division fought a series of skirmishes throughout 29 August, hard pressed by the German XX and XVII corps, as Francois' I Corps cut off any escape due south. A Russian staff conference a mile short of Muschaken at 7 p.m. acknowledged that the Germans held this village and opted to attempt a break-out through the forest between Yanou and Chorzele. The German I Corps had, however, anticipated this and mounted guns along the Neidenburg–Willenburg road to cover exits from the woods. Casualties from artillery fire within the forest frequently blocked the narrow tracks in whose glutinous mud field guns and supply wagons stuck fast adding to the Russians' misery. Treacherous swamps, ponds and wider lakes further hampered progress and cohesion. With their infantry unable to cross the open ground in any significant numbers to attack the Germans, the Russians decided instead to make for Willenburg, unaware that it had fallen. At Rettkowen, 6 miles north-east of Muschaken, the worn-out men of the XV and XXIII corps were surrounded and the bulk of them surrendered – the first total disaster for the Russians, but not the last. Two small contingents managed to evade capture. Baron Stempel led part of the 6th Cavalry Division and an artillery battery, acquiring an isolated divisional commander en route, broke through the German cordon west of Willenburg and reached Chorzele during the morning of 30 August. The second group, comprising fifteen officers and 1,200 men of the 31st Alexis Regiment under Colonel Suchachevski, evaded German troops in Puchallowen and safely crossed the frontier during the night of 29–30 August.

Meanwhile, having ridden through the previous night, at first light on 29 August Martos and his staff found themselves 4 miles north-east of Neidenburg. Taking cover in a convenient wood, they learned from a patrol that the town had already fallen to the Germans. At this point Lieutenant General Torklus arrived, and conveyed the false impression that the 6th Division was behind him in good order. When these troops arrived, Martos planned to divert them to the Neidenburg–Yanou road. Believing that friendly units were ahead, the corps commander emerged from the wood to reconnoitre the new position, which he had chosen from a map. A German position fewer than 1,000 yards distant promptly opened fire, killing several of his Cossack escort. Martos, his staff officers and six Cossacks managed to reach cover to reassess the situation. The promised orderly 6th Division did not appear. With shells peppering the forest, Martos remained there until afternoon, when he ventured out towards Yanou. Perhaps deliberately misdirected by two Polish peasants, the party was swept by two dug-in machine guns. Casualties included the XV Corps Chief of Staff, leaving Martos with one sick officer and two Cossacks to regain the wood. There they hid until nightfall, while German patrols scoured the nearby undergrowth for them. Having lost his ADC and his haversack containing food and water during the last mêlée, as darkness fell a hungry and thirsty Martos led off his small party guided by the stars. Cloud soon obscured the sky, however; one horse dropped dead with fatigue and, hearing troops in the vicinity, a Cossack went to investigate. He did not return. As the depleted group approached the village of Modlken, near Muschaken, a searchlight picked it out and Martos galloped into cover followed by a burst of rifle fire. He was then shot at from behind bushes, his horse went down, and he was taken prisoner lying breathless on the ground. The XV Corps commander would spend the rest of the war in captivity.

In the meantime, Klyuev's XIII Corps had trudged onward through that blistering late summer's day, at 7 p.m. reaching Jablonken on the western shore of Lake Omulefoten – tired and hungry. Neither men nor horses had been fed for two days. Their orders were to reach Muschaken by the morning of 30 August. After a short rest, therefore, they pressed on. As night closed in on 29 August, the Russian XIII Corps entered Kummusin Forest. There it came across some of the XV Corps driven from Lahna, which were trying to catch up with the main body unaware that it had already surrendered, and elements of the XXIII Corps. Much valuable time was lost in sorting out the confusion, before the XIII Corps with the other partial corps following separately moved off towards Kaltenborn. At this stage the XIII Corps had marched 42 miles in forty hours.

Of the Russian Second Army, at midnight on 29 August only the XIII Corps retained any sort of reasonable cohesion, though the I and VI corps had not altogether disintegrated. But these three corps were isolated from one another; except in Zhilinski's distant HQ all thoughts of a co-ordinated strategy had vanished. Francois' control of the road from Neidenburg to Willenburg posed a major problem for troops attempting to recross the southern frontier of East Prussia, as Klyuev and Martos had painfully discovered. Now in Warsaw, Knox noted: 'Common report is that the Germans were pushed back by a flank attack and that they suffered enormous loss'. Sceptically and wisely, he added: 'I hope that this is true!'[36]

For, in reality, the facts made much less comfortable reading for Russian eyes. After giving further orders to secure Hohenstein, Hindenburg and Ludendorff travelled there, in the Chief of Staff's words 'to try and disentangle the congestion caused by the troops getting mixed up', a consequence of so many men converging on that area. Nevertheless, the situation was heartening for the Germans. The I Reserve and XX corps were largely intact in the Allenstein–Hohenstein region, the 3rd Reserve Division had reached Muschaken east of Neidenburg to meet I Corps in firm control of the road from Neidenburg to Willenburg. Hindenburg, though, paid tribute to Russian 'heroism, which saved the honour of arms, but could no longer save the battle'.[37]

**Resting German infantry** watch supply units pass on their way to the front during the battle of Tannenberg.

At 10 p.m. on 29 August the Eighth Army commander informed 'the troops entrusted to me by H.M. the Kaiser' that 'the enemy has been decisively beaten and has been dispersed', expressing to them 'the deepest gratitude for their supreme efforts in marching and fighting'.[38]

The measure of confusion which existed at Russian staff level may be gauged by the experience of Gurko's cavalry division. At 3 p.m. on 29 August, as he and his staff were sitting down to lunch, a staff officer from the First Army HQ arrived by car with an order for Gurko to co-operate with other cavalry divisions in an advance on Allenstein, because no communication had been received from Samsonov for two days. Conscious of the previous day's clash with German formations, he realized that this meant having to 'cut our way through territory in enemy hands'.[39] At 7 p.m. Zhilinski told Rennenkampf to reinforce the cavalry divisions with two infantry corps, steadfastly maintaining that the Second Army had advanced in good order and not disintegrated. When more accurate intelligence revealed in the evening the true, disastrous position, at 11 p.m. the operation was called off. Gurko could not be contacted, however, before his departure at midnight. Quite unsupported, therefore, his fifteen and a half squadrons, six machine guns and a battery of six 3-inch field guns pressed on southwards through the darkness. Gurko knew that to reach his destination meant negotiating over 30 miles of enemy-held territory and crossing several defended railway lines.

## 30 AUGUST

The day did not start auspiciously for the Russian Second Army. Klyuev divided his remaining troops into three columns: the right-hand one would make for Muschaken; in the centre, in person he would lead that column to Saddek; the left-hand one was to go to Wallendorf. However, unknown to the XIII Corps commander, Mackensen's German XVII Corps was tightening the net from the north. The central column came under intense fire and suffered severe casualties; many became prisoners (including Klyuev) and ultimately surrendered short of Saddek. A Russian staff officer described the end: 'Disorganised by the firing upon them, with the column broken up into separate detachments, units were either annihilated piecemeal or captured'. The left-hand column also ran into serious trouble, but fought strenuously throughout 30 August, several times rebuffing German attacks and capturing twenty guns, without, as Ludendorff observed, 'in any way influencing the issue of the battle'. By midnight, although in a perilous state, Russian survivors were still hanging on, hoping for relief. It had been a frustrating day, as one participant recorded: 'Whenever our units took the offensive, the Germans

## Tannenberg, 29–30 August

Russian army p

Russian attack

Russian withdra

German counte

German army p

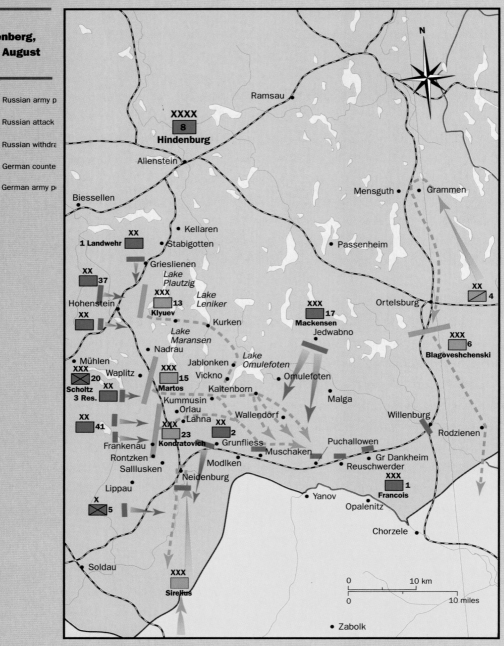

N

Ramsau

XXXX
8
**Hindenburg**

Allenstein

Mensguth • Grammen

Biessellen

Kellaren

**1 Landwehr** XX     • Stabigotten

Grieslienen

Passenheim

XX 37

*Lake Plautzig*

Hohenstein

XXX 13
**Klyuev**

*Lake Leniker*

• Kurken

Ortelsburg

XX 4

XX

*Lake Maransen*

• Nadrau

XXX 17
**Mackensen**

Jedwabno

XXX 6
**Blagoveshchenski**

• Mühlen

Jablonken

*Lake Omulefoten*

Waplitz

XXX 20
**Scholtz 3 Res.**

XXX 15
**Martos**

Vickno

• Omulefoten

Kaltenborn

• Malga

XX 41

Kummusin

Orlau

Lahna

Wallendorf

Willenburg

Frankenau

XXX 23
**Kondratovich**

XX 2

Grunfliess

Muschaken

Puchallowen

Rodzienen

Rontzken

Sallusken

Modlken

Gr Dankheim

Reuschwerder

Lippau

Neidenburg

XXX 1
**Francois**

X 5

• Yanov

Opalenitz

Soldau

• Chorzele

XXX
**Sirelius**

0          10 km

0          10 miles

• Zabolk

without meeting the charge would roll their line back, and bring out attacking units under their machine guns'.[40] The Germans, though, also suffered hardship, with supplies of food difficult to obtain and worn out troops sleeping in fields in their greatcoats. At Reuschwerder, Lieutenant Heeder admitted later, 'The Russians were putting up white flags, but we took no notice and shot them because we feared it was a ruse. Eventually, they came towards us with a very large white flag' as a Russian officer told his men to lay down their arms. This time the surrender was accepted and 20,000 prisoners were taken. The many officers were put in farmhouses, their men left in open fields. Ludendorff would subsequently angrily react to suggestions that prisoners were deliberately maltreated: 'The widely-circulated report that thousands of Russians were driven into the marshes and there perished is a myth'.[41]

On the German right, at 9.15 a.m. a message was dropped into Neidenburg square from a reconnaissance aeroplane, reporting aerial observations during the past half-hour: 'Column of all arms moving from Mlawa on Neidenburg. Head at Kandien, tail one kilometre N. of Mlawa … a second column moving from Stupsk on Mlawa. Head at E. entrance of Mlawa, tail Wola'. Kandien was

**Surrender.**
At the end of August 1914, during the battle of Tannenberg, large pockets of troops from the Russian Second Army were surrounded and forced to surrender. This scene illustrates one such episode.

just 3 miles south of Neidenburg; Mlawa 20 miles to the south-west, too far for its troops to pose immediate danger. Kandien presented a much more acute problem. Ordered by Samsonov to recapture Neidenburg, now commanding the XXIII Corps Lieutenant General Sirelius had gathered fifteen battalions of the Russian 3rd Guard Division and the 1st Rifle Brigade together with six batteries of field artillery and part of the 6th Cavalry Division to march north from Mlawa at 6 p.m. on 29 August. This was the leading force spotted from the air.

The Germans had written off an attack from this direction, but the I Corps commander (Francois) reacted quickly, realizing the need for positive action to preserve control of the road to Willenburg and his stranglehold on the Russians' southern escape route. He sent verbal orders by a staff officer for the detachment of troops under Major Schlimm, holding a rise halfway between Neidenburg and Kandien, to delay attackers long enough for the 2nd Division at Grunfliess to march east of Neidenburg and hit the Russian right flank. Simultaneously, moving south-east from Soldau, Mülmann would attack the left flank. Alerted by a similar message from the reconnaissance machine, Ludendorff at the Eighth Army HQ ordered Goltz's Landwehr Division, the 3rd Reserve Division, a detachment under Major General Unger and a division each from the XVII and the XX corps to assist Francois, knowing that the Russian XIII Corps had been broken. Before reinforcements arrived, however, the southern detachment north of Kandien had been overrun and Sirelius reoccupied Neidenburg; in Russian records during the afternoon, according to the Germans at 9 p.m. Meanwhile, during that morning, Martos had seen the town under heavy bombardment as he was driven away by car into captivity. Explaining that Russian troops from Mühlen to Hohenstein had surrendered, a German staff officer suggested that Martos might act as an intermediary to stop the unnecessary bloodshed. However, the idea was discarded once it became clear that Martos' personal safety could not be guaranteed.

The struggle for Neidenburg inevitably weakened the German hold on the road to Willenburg, and this benefited the right-hand column of Klyuev's

Russian XIII Corps making for Muschaken. As a result an estimated 170 officers and 13,300 men escaped across the frontier; encouraging, but in truth a paltry tally. On the Russian right, survivors of the VI Corps had spent 29 August consolidating south of Ortelsburg, which had fallen to the Germans. A half-hearted effort by Blagoveshchenski to retake the town during the morning of 30 August failed, and shortly afterwards Zhilinski ordered the Corps to Willenburg. There in co-operation with the XXIII Corps (about to surrender) it was to protect Samsonov's right flank and his lines of communication. Another pipe dream. Zhilinski added that the I Corps had been ordered to recapture Neidenburg. Contact had been lost with Samsonov, but he was believed to be somewhere in the (vast) Hohenstein/Neidenburg/Jedwabno area, where a pilot was searching for him to deliver fresh orders from the North-West Front commander. Blagoveshchenski seemed unimpressed by this vague scenario. Instead of moving south-west to Willenburg, he deployed the 4th Cavalry Division on his left and withdrew his main force south-east along the road to Myszyniec over the frontier, reaching Radzienen that evening. 'Our ring of fire round the Russian masses crowded close together … became closer and narrower with every hour that passed', Hindenburg observed.[42]

The reason for Zhilinski's inability to raise Samsonov became apparent later. Leaving Orlau, he and his small party set off for Yanou, only to find every road and track blocked by jostling transport. He therefore headed for Willenburg, hoping to contact Blagoveshchenski. On the way Samsonov's group ran into several German detachments, charging one of which the Cossack escort was wiped out. Nearing Willenburg with only seven officers and one NCO, Samsonov learned that the Germans were there. He therefore decided to rest in a wood and slip away to the south during darkness, which would mean moving on foot; considerable hardship for a man with breathing problems, who had been on sick leave at the outbreak of war. Already he had intimated to his Chief of Staff Postovski that he was feeling the physical strain. As night fell, the trek began in unpromising circumstances: no maps, one compass and a few matches with which to see it.

Meanwhile, that morning Gurko had ploughed his lonely furrow towards Allenstein. At 6 a.m. he had his first brush with German infantry as he crossed a railway line, which caused an hour's hold-up, recording that 'I had not the slightest information about the enemy in this district, because it was remote from our base of operations'. Nor had he any news of the friendly forces, which he believed were accompanying him. Continuing to overcome light opposition, destroying railway lines, telegraph and telephone links as the force rode on, shortly before midday Gurko recorded that 'in the distance the buildings and barracks in Allenstein could be seen with the naked eye'. Hopes of a friendly reception were soon dashed, though. Scouts dispatched to contact a mythical hussar regiment on grey horses found only aggressive German opposition. 'There was much swearing', Cornet Littauer laconically observed.[43] Then, 'soon after noon', German infantry emerged from the town to engage dismounted lancers in Gurko's vanguard followed swiftly by salvoes of shells, which began pitching uncomfortably among the horses of the main Russian concentration. It dawned on Gurko not only that strong hostile forces were ahead of him, but that none of the promised cavalry nor infantry were behind him. Moreover, with 'barely more than 1,500 dismounted rifles', he feared being outflanked. 'About 3pm, having travelled more than 50km [31 miles] according to the map, having fought several small engagements at the railways, and a more serious fight before the town of Allenstein itself, and not having seen any signs at all of the Russian troops … I felt that I had done all that was possible'. He therefore ordered a withdrawal. Littauer, who was with the hussar rearguard, described (in a retrospective graphic account timed throughout twenty-four hours later than the correct sequence of events), how the force slowly withdrew that evening and was harassed throughout the night. Hampered by thick forest, deep streams and ravines in their path, as their pursuers played searchlights along prominent roads, according to Littauer they managed only 5.5 miles in three hours at one stage; many 'of our men remained in their saddles fast asleep, with their faces buried in their horses' manes'. However, the hussars were sent along the line of Gurko's advance to Allenstein to dupe the Germans. Gurko's main body went further east, which allowed a halt for rest and food between 6 and 11 p.m. Resuming the march, Gurko's vanguard lost its way and incurred losses after stumbling into a defended village. Eventually, though, the main force extricated itself and continued to withdraw.[44]

## 31 AUGUST

Only the loose ends of the Russian Second Army's failure remained to be tied up. By dawn its commander was dead. At 1 a.m. a short halt in the progress of Samsonov's tiny band through the thick forest was called. With the stars obscured by foliage and, the matches having run out, no means of consulting the compass, the direction followed owed much to guesswork. To avoid losing contact with one another, the men were reduced to holding hands, as the Second Army commander according to his Chief of Staff kept muttering, 'The tsar trusted me', and doubting whether he could bear to face Nicholas II again.[45] When the time came to resume the march, Samsonov could not be found. A shot was heard, and a brief unsuccessful search conducted for the Army commander. With dawn fast approaching and German patrols in the vicinity, the rest of the party led by Postovski set off once more and shortly after daylight a Cossack patrol guided it across the frontier. Hopes that Samsonov might have evaded the Germans were ultimately dashed. A German patrol found his body with a single gunshot wound, identifying it by the medallion he wore. Depressed and exhausted, he had committed suicide; though the spectre of a noble sacrifice to avoid slowing down the party endures. The Germans buried Samsonov, whose body was later retrieved and reinterred in the family vault.

Martos, after being driven away from Neidenburg, met Hindenburg and Ludendorff at their HQ in Osterode, rather a scruffy inn according to their captive. The German Eighth Army commander was more friendly than his abrupt Chief of Staff, promising to return the ornamental sword presented to

Martos after the Russo-Japanese War and expressing sympathy for his predicament. Unbeknown to either man, that would soon worsen appreciably. While imprisoned in Germany Martos was accused of bombarding an undefended town (Neidenburg on 22 August), causing casualties among innocent civilians including women and children. The penalty on conviction for this alleged crime was death, and an agonizing six months passed before Martos was acquitted.

**Tannenberg,
26–31 August – overview**

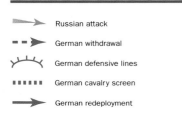

Russian attack

German withdrawal

German defensive lines

German cavalry screen

German redeployment

For the Germans 31 August represented 'the day of the harvesting'.[46] Surrounded, hungry and greatly outnumbered, during the morning Klyuev's left-hand column trying to reach Wallendorf surrendered. As they did so, having heard of the other disasters and being under attack from right and left, without waiting for specific orders Sirelius skilfully extricated his troops from Neidenburg – and was later dismissed for doing so, although after an enquiry he was subsequently cleared of all blame. This Russian withdrawal did not altogether quieten German nerves. While driving through Neidenburg square later that day a traffic policeman shouted that Lieutenant General von Morgen's car contained Russians, prompting a volley from nearby troops which killed the driver. That night, sleeping in Modlken, the 3rd Reserve Division commander was rudely awakened by a false warning that Russian troops were in the village. Elsewhere, as the hopeless situation at last dawned on him, Zhilinski cancelled previous aggressive orders and instructed all troops to withdraw across the frontier.

The picture was infinitely brighter for the Germans. Hindenburg could 'humbly' inform Wilhelm II that three Russian corps had been annihilated, the commanders of the XIII and XV Corps captured to date together with 60,000 other prisoners. In addition, 'the booty is immense though it cannot yet be assessed in detail'. Admitting that much of the Russian I and VI corps had escaped, nevertheless they had 'suffered heavily and are now retreating in hot haste through Mlawa and Myszyniec'.[47] The final total of casualties,

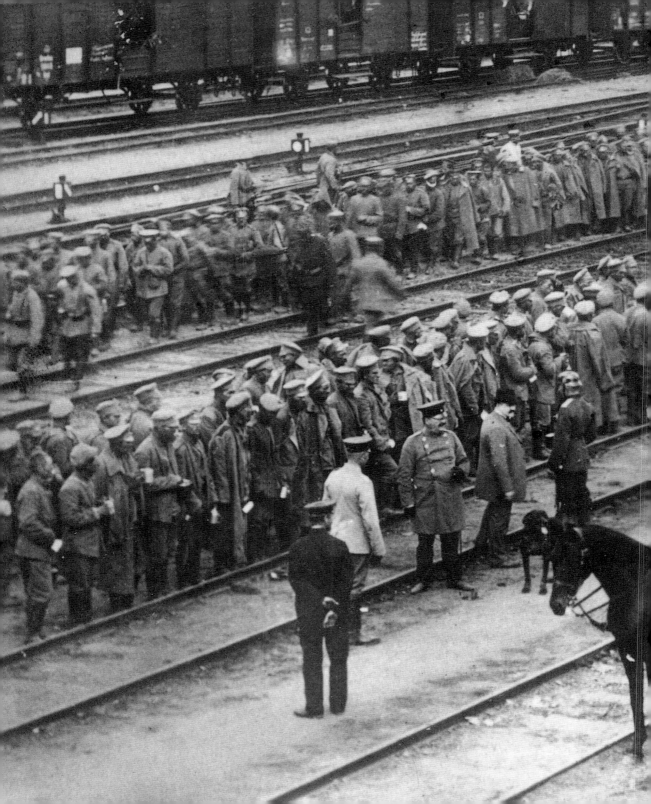

**Captivity.** Russian soldiers waiting for trains to take them to prisoner of war camps.

although admittedly vast, was disputed. Later German sources claimed 170,000 Russian dead, wounded and captured, at a cost of 10,000–15,000 German casualties, and 500 guns taken. At the time Hoffmann noted 92,000 prisoners. The Russians detailed 60,000 prisoners, 70,000 casualties and 180–190 guns lost. In reality the overall difference was largely irrelevant; inescapably the Russian Second Army had been routed. In the Protestant church at Allenstein, which the Eighth Army commander reflected was close to an old Teutonic castle, Hindenburg and Ludendorff 'rendered thanks to Almighty God for this victory'. Ludendorff described Tannenberg as 'one of the most brilliant battles in the history of the world', about which 'the world was silent'. Despite an overall inferiority of numbers in East Prussia, the Germans had assembled against Samsonov a force of roughly equal strength and beaten him. Ludendorff was 'proud', and 'exceedingly' so when he received the Iron Cross, Second Class, for his part in the triumph; 'my heart swells with pardonable satisfaction'. Hindenburg noted that 'the hymn of thanks of the Battle of Leuthen rose from their [German] ranks' – another reminder of the nation's military tradition. In retrospect, Hoffmann believed that Tannenberg would have been won without a change of command, but not so completely. 'Former experiences had shown' that Prittwitz and Waldersee 'did not possess the necessary energy'; a damning indictment.[48]

Gurko's cavalry division, after its abortive excursion to Allenstein, did not figure in the statistics of disaster. By noon on 31 August it had covered 62 miles in thirty-six hours and was resting when reports came in that columns of German infantry were approaching after realizing that they had been fooled by the detour of Gurko's main force. Gurko decided that 'the extreme weariness of my troops, especially of the artillery horses, made it impossible to give battle', so he moved off north-eastwards with his troopers driving their exhausted horses in front of them like cattle. As fire to the rear revealed that another German column had moved up to engage the retreating Russians, Gurko reluctantly prepared to fight when 'a deluge of rain fell and completely hid us from the enemy'. By the time that it stopped Gurko's men had escaped.

# B·Z· am Mittag

In Groß-Berlin 5 Pf.

Nr. 204
Berliner Zeitung
38. Jahrgang

Verlag Ullstein & Co. – Redaktion: Berlin SW 68, Kochstraße 22–25. Abonnement: Monatlich 1,20 M. In Berlin frei ins Haus. Außerhalb bei der Post. Zusendung unter Streifband wöchentlich 60 Pfennig, Ausland 90 Pfennig. Einzelnummer 5 Pfennig, außerhalb 10 Pfennig.

Anzeigen: Die sechsgespaltene Nonparelle · Zeile 75 Pfennig, Reklamezeile 5 Mark. Annahmeschluß für Anzeigen am Tage zuvor bis 6 Uhr abends. Telegramm-Adresse: Ullsteinhaus Berlin, Telephon-Zentrale: Ullstein & Co. Amt Moritzplatz, Nr. 11800 bis 11845.

1 Uhr
Sonnabend
29. August 1914

# Freudenbotschaft aus Ostpreußen:

## Fünf russische Armeekorps geschlagen.

Wolffs Telegraphen-Bureau meldet amtlich:

Berlin, 29. August.

Unsere Truppen in Preußen unter Führung des Generalobersten von Hindenburg haben die vom Narew vorgegangene russische Armee in der Stärke von fünf Armeekorps und drei Kavalleriedivisionen in dreitägiger Schlacht in der Gegend von Gilgenburg und Ortelsburg geschlagen und verfolgen sie jetzt über die Grenze.

Der Generalquartiermeister
von Stein.

**Victory.**
A German declaration on 29 August 1914 claiming that five Russian army corps had been defeated in the battle of Tannenberg under the heading 'Glad Tidings from East Prussia'.

Once again safely in friendly lines at 6 p.m., Gurko learned that messengers sent to recall him on the morning of 30 August had been frustrated by German patrols: 'I recognise that we only managed to execute this "dash through" and get safely back by sheer luck'. Not many other Russian units had such fortune that day.[49]

Nevertheless, in their hour of triumph the Germans could not afford to relax. 'It was an uncommonly difficult task simultaneously to finish one battle and make plans for the next', in Ludendorff's eyes. The six-day battle had ranged over much of the southern part of East Prussia. Ludendorff afterwards wrote that he suggested it be named the Battle of Tannenberg 'in memory of that other battle long ago in which the Teutonic Knights succumbed to the united Lithuanian and Polish hosts'. A counter-claim, however, credits Hoffmann with that suggestion, Ludendorff having opted for Frögenau, site of the Eighth Army HQ. More immediately, Hoffmann recorded in his diary that Tannenberg constituted 'a fine revenge of Gumbinnen ... [though] we have not been able to destroy quite the entire horde'.[50]

Defeat of the Russian Second Army had not ended the threat to East Prussia. Rennenkampf's First Army had still to be faced: Gurko's northward retreat served to underline this fact. Lieutenant Heeder relished the challenge: 'I hope we have a new battle soon as I am sure we shall be victorious'. Hoffmann wrote, 'one entire army is disposed of: now for the other'.[51]

## RUSSIAN FIRST ARMY REVITALIZED

At 9 a.m. on 31 August the Russian North-West Front HQ reported to GHQ that the Second Army had suffered severe setbacks and therefore was no longer advancing as planned; but it fell short of acknowledging disaster. The confusion reigning among Zhilinski's staff at Volkovisk was further underlined later that day, when another message to Baranovichi admitted 'no information' about where the Second Army's separate corps were. Nevertheless, 'it can be assumed' that the I Corps 'is fighting at Neidenburg ... VI Corps is between Willenburg and Myszyniec'. There was 'no news of the XIII corps ... [but] men of the XV Corps are arriving in batches at Ostrolenka'. Some of the XXIII Corps were 'fighting' with the I Corps, others with the XV Corps; 'the remnants' were reorganizing in Russian Poland, south of the border.[1]

On the basis of this information, which did not reveal the true extent of the Second Army's plight, GHQ issued revised orders on 31 August. 'At all costs' First Army should maintain its position north of the Masurian Lakes and Zhilinski must strongly garrison the fortress of Novo Georgievsk, between Mlawa and Warsaw, in the south. 'Gradually reorganising', the Second Army was to retire to the line Sokola–Osowiec–Lomza. 'Without sparing itself', the cavalry must cover this withdrawal, then reform on the left flank and carry out reconnaissance towards Thorn and the Lower Vistula. The XXII Finnish, III Siberian and I Turkestan corps, destined to form the new Tenth Army and ordered to the Narew area, would be transferred to Zhilinski's command with the aim of reinforcing the Second Army. Meanwhile, defences were to be prepared along the Niemen, Bobr and Upper Narew rivers. With the First Army still in possession of roughly half East Prussia, the North-West Front was now to act defensively, resist and contain the German troops in front of it.[2]

Having reached Ostrowo, Major General Postovski (Samsonov's Chief of Staff) learned that he had been placed in temporary charge of the Second Army, because its commander's whereabouts was then unknown. GHQ repeated Zhilinski's assertion that the I Corps 'is fighting at Neidenburg' and ordered Postovski to withdraw it to Mlawa 'otherwise it may come in contact with superior forces'. Postovski was reminded that 'it is of the utmost importance to get the units organised, fed and brought into rest'. The message from Baranovichi concluded with a plea and a forlorn hope. 'Try to get information as to where the XIII Corps is. Isolated men must certainly turn up in large numbers'.[3] Postovski had scant opportunity to respond. Before the day was out, Lieutenant General Scheidemann of the II Corps had been appointed to command the Second Army.

Meanwhile, strengthened by the XXVI Corps (53rd and 56th reserve divisions), Rennenkampf had eight and a half first-line infantry divisions on German soil, five reserve already there or preparing to arrive and two reserve divisions behind the Niemen; a total of fifteen and a half divisions. However, being outflanked from the south was a clear possibility, because the XXII Finnish,

III Siberian and I Turkestan corps were not due in the line until 12 September.

A series of significant signals passed between the First Army and North-West Front during 31 August. Lieutenant General Oranovski, Zhilinski's Chief of Staff, urged the First Army to 'take every measure to destroy railway lines', which the Germans might employ, and to ensure that the enemy were unable to 'operate against you in the Lötzen direction'. Recognizing the need to consolidate the First Army's defences, its Chief of Staff (Mileant) wired Oranovski for permission to retire eastwards beyond Insterburg and draw back the left flank corps behind Goldap. Mileant claimed that Nahichevanski's cavalry at Landsberg had already inflicted 'serious damage on the railway stations in the neighbourhood'; other cavalry under Lieutenant General Raukh were at Friedland, Gurko in the process of moving south from Heinrichsdorf to Passenheim. Oranovski supported Mileant's proposal to concentrate on a more stable defence line and further agreed that the outlying cavalry units should be brought back into touch with the main force.[4]

These plans survived scarcely an hour. Rennenkampf rejected withdrawal of the infantry as bad for morale; though he did sanction an entrenched division facing Lötzen as a screen. He declined to call back the cavalry; effectively therefore vetoing his Chief of Staff's agreement with Oranovski. A First Army staff officer commented that 'Rennenkampf is a very peculiar man; he has no love for the General Staff'. Moreover, he scarcely communicated with Mileant and relied heavily on Gurko, who had been his Chief of Staff in Manchuria.[5]

The Germans had no intention of allowing the Russians to dictate static warfare. A potentially serious complication arose, however, as Hindenburg and Ludendorff drew up their plans. Hard pressed by Russian forces further south in Galicia, Austria–Hungary requested a German supportive attack from East Prussia. Hindenburg was conscious that any such move would not only put Königsberg in peril but invite the Russian First Army to disrupt the lines of communication of any German force conducting such a campaign. Ludendorff agreed that 'there was no alternative but to deal first with the Russian Niemen Army'.[6]

**German trenches at Lötzen.**
Despite Russian pressure and a summons to surrender, the fortress of Lötzen covering a crucial gap between the Masurian Lakes held firm. This allowed German forces to attack the flank of the Russian First Army.

Despite his insistence that the cavalry continue to range widely, Rennenkampf neither mounted specific reconnaissance patrols nor ordered determined aerial surveillance. In the days immediately prior to 30 August he redeployed his forces. Pivoting on the II Corps at Angerburg, three corps (north to south, the XX, III and IV) were moved to the line Nordenburg–Allenburg. Rennenkampf sent two cavalry brigades south of Lötzen, and another three advanced on Königsberg only to be held up at the Deime river. Fort Boyen covering the Lötzen gap, from which the garrison had launched irritating sorties in the past, remained a burr on the Russian line. The First Army commander therefore ordered his 170th Regiment, supported by four guns and a detachment of Cossacks, to deal with it. On 27 August a II Corps staff officer, orderly and trumpeter rode forward to invite the garrison commander to surrender within four hours or 'not one stone will be left upon another'.[7] A volley of rifle fire, which wounded two of the party and led to their capture, was the instant response. Lötzen survived to provide an invaluable exit through which German troops would soon pour to attack the Russian left flank.

Rennenkampf's plans were further disrupted by Zhilinski, who at 7 p.m. on 29 August required the First Army commander to move two of his infantry corps with the cavalry divisions already ordered south that afternoon to support Samsonov. Four hours later, accepting that the Second Army's advance had petered out, he cancelled the order (an alteration of plan which failed to reach Gurko). The North-West Front commander then proposed to send the II Corps via Suwalki, Bialystok and Ostrolenka to reinforce the Second Army, only to be persuaded that a 90 mile march followed by 160 miles by train would put it out of action for at least two weeks. The following day, 30 August, Zhilinski warned Rennenkampf that 'General Samsonov had suffered a complete defeat, and the enemy has now complete liberty to turn against you', again reminding him that German troops could easily debouch from the Lötzen Gap. At the time of the exchanges with GHQ on 31 August, the First Army's two right-hand infantry corps (XXVI and XX) lay near the Baltic close to Königsberg; the left-hand (II) covering defiles through the Masurian Lakes, supported by the 76th reserve division. In the centre, the III and IV corps were entrenched in the Insterburg Gap, behind the Pregel river and 20 miles west of Insterburg. Noting the strong forces at the Russian commander's disposal, Hindenburg observed 'yet he stood still and remained thus, while our army came up from the west and deployed for battle against him'.[8]

Even before GHQ's directive to assume a defensive posture, basically Rennenkampf wanted to stand on ground of his own choosing between Wehlau on the Pregel river and Lake Mauer. He believed that his position behind the rivers Omet, Alle and Deime with clear fields of fire for his entrenched units was strong; Zhilinski had promised to reinforce his southern flank with the embryo Tenth Army. On 4 September Zhilinski told

Rennenkampf that a German offensive was anticipated along the southern frontier towards Mlawa, so that 'it appears necessary to assume an offensive against East Prussia',[9] drastically revising the orders for a defensive posture issued five days previously. Perhaps Rennenkampf's suspicion of the General Staff was not unreasonable. Zhilinski seems not to have suspected that the Germans would switch their axis once more to the north, expecting them to follow up the beaten Russian Second Army. The reported advance on Mlawa further misled him.

Thus, on 4 September, Zhilinski informed Rennenkampf that the XXII Finnish and III Siberian corps would be put under his command. However, he placed the onus of deciding on the feasibility of offensive action on the First Army commander. 'If you consider it possible to assume the offensive with the forces at your disposal, and for the two corps mentioned to come up by stages on your left flank, I sanction your assuming the offensive in the Bischofstein–Rastenburg direction [south south-west of Insterburg and west of the Masurian Lakes], after taking the necessary measures to safeguard yourself from attack from the direction of Königsberg'. The only explanation for this suggestion is that the North-West Front staff was still thinking in terms of some sort of double envelopment despite all that had happened in the previous week.

The following day, 5 September, after consulting GHQ, Zhilinski's fancy took wing and he issued more detailed orders: Rennenkampf no longer had flexibility of decision. 'The leading units of the XXII Finnish and III Siberian corps had already been despatched to the Lyck area',[10] and the North-West Front commander confirmed that together with the III Siberian Corps they would ultimately form Tenth Army. The proposed division between First and Tenth armies would be the southern shore of Lake Lowentin–Widminnen –Marggrabowa; between Tenth and Second armies Russchanni–Chijev.

Incredibly, Zhilinski proceeded to envisage a general offensive by all three armies on 14 September; the First Army being required to capture Lötzen prior to that date. Apart from the unrealistic assumption that the Masurian Lake fortress could now be taken after repeated failures, the Tenth Army could not assemble in any sort of shape before 18 September. This possibly explains why on 4 September Zhilinski put two of its corps under Rennenkampf. Furthermore, there seemed no logical reason to assume that the Second Army would be in any condition to renew hostilities with the Germans. These pronouncements were castles in the sky.

On 7 September Rennenkampf learned that the Germans were advancing eastwards towards him on a wide front, and the North-West Front HQ told him that one (not the actual two) new infantry corps from France had been identified. Unaccountably, that day Zhilinski also informed the First Army commander that the Second Army was again advancing on Neidenburg. He further encouraged Rennenkampf with news that more Tenth Army troops were detraining prior to tackling the German right flank near Bialla. At the same time, Zhilinski renewed his propensity for nagging by re-emphasizing that the First Army's left flank remained weak.

On 31 August the German GHQ at Koblenz signalled that the Guards Reserve and XI corps, together with the 8th Cavalry Division, were being sent from the Western Front, adding: 'The first task of the Eighth Army is to clear East Prussia of Rennenkampf's army'. The commander of the German Eighth Army and his Chief of Staff lost no time in redeploying their corps, although Russian cavalry patrols were reported as far west as the Passarge river below Wormditt. To Ludendorff's relief, despite Russian claims to the contrary they caused no significant damage to the railways, which Ludendorff underlined were of 'utmost importance'.[11]

## GERMAN REDEPLOYMENT

The Eighth Army HQ intended to attack Rennenkampf's main concentration north of the Lakes on a broad front between the Pregel river and Lake Mauer, while the German right wing swept through convenient defiles between them and south of the Lakes. Other troops would guard against an advance of newly arrived Russian troops from beyond the frontier; for Hindenburg worried

**On guard.** The Masurian Lake complex ran roughly north-south for 60 miles through the centre of East Prussia. Several of the larger lakes were navigable and German positions like this guarded against a Russian attack across the water.

about 'what the enemy had by way of dark secrets in the region south-east of the Masurian Lakes'. By 4 September preparations were well in hand, and three days later the Germans were poised to attack the Russian First Army. In the Eighth Army commander's words, 'we had to be cautious and bold',[12] because retirement of an undefeated Rennenkampf would undermine plans to support the Austrians in the south. He remained puzzled as to why, even when the Germans came clearly into sight, Rennenkampf made no effort to interfere with their movements.

With the Eighth Army HQ now at Allenstein, the German line stretched approximately 130 miles between Wehlau and Soldau. On its left flank, the Königsberg Main Reserve would hold the line of the Deime river to counter any northern outflanking move. In the centre was the Guards Reserve Corps at Preussisch-Eylau; the I Reserve Corps with the 6th Landwehr Brigade were at Heilsburg; the XI and XX corps respectively at Seeburg and Wartenburg were ranged roughly from north to south along the line Wehlau–Gerdauen–Ordenburg–Angerburg facing 'strong and cleverly constructed' Russian positions. Hindenburg recorded evidence of 'a good deal of movement' behind the Russian front, concluding that 'Rennenkampf had undoubtedly received reinforcements'.[13] In the south, the XVII Corps at Mensguth was ready to advance through the Lötzen Gap; the I Corps near Ortelsburg from Nikolaiken and Johannisburg to sweep round the southern edge of the Masurian Lakes, with the 8th Cavalry Division on its left and the 1st Cavalry Division on its right scouting ahead. The 3rd Reserve Division at Friedrichshof, supported by Goltz's Landwehr division and the 70th Landwehr Brigade, would cover the south-east frontier, aware that fresh Russian formations had appeared in the Augustow and Osowiec area. Documents captured during the Battle of Tannenberg had warned of plans for new divisions to converge on Grodno. On the extreme right (south-west) Mülmann with his Landwehr brigade and troops from the Vistula garrisons in the region of Soldau safeguarded the German rear areas and lines of communication, at the same time watching the road and rail links from Warsaw via Mlawa. Ordered to carry out a raid

over the frontier, these men were apparently instrumental in convincing Zhilinski that a major thrust on Mlawa was imminent. One division was initially retained immediately west of the Lakes as a mobile reserve, but later rejoined the XX Corps. Ludendorff argued that the whole operation was extraordinarily daring.

The Germans estimated that Rennenkampf had 'about two divisions' in his right wing facing their troops along the Deime river, with 'about three Army Corps' from there on the line Gerdauen–Drengfurth south to Lake Mauer, the 'weaker' left wing of the Russian First Army extending eastwards past Lötzen with detachments at Arys and Johannisburg.[14] During the lull in fighting on this front, they learned that the Russians had vastly strengthened their field

**German Cavalry on the move.**
Exploitation of land corridors between stretches of water and swamp became critical during the battle of the Masurian Lakes. These German cavalry take advantage of one such route.

defences. Only slightly inaccurately Hoffmann calculated, without knowing their precise details, that Rennenkampf had four divisions in reserve; and that the XXII Finnish Corps was about to come into the line in the south-east. The Eighth Army would attack along the whole of this Russian front.

## GERMAN OFFENSIVE

On 8 September, just nine days after the death throes of the Russian Second Army, in Hindenburg's words the battle of the Masurian Lakes 'blazed up'; although preliminary skirmishes had already signalled the coming conflict. Russian outposts on the Deime river were attacked during the night of 6–7 September. With reports of German movement in the south-east, the 3rd Finnish Rifle Brigade at Bialla was rapidly reinforced, to no avail; eight battalions and four batteries of artillery were no match for the Germans, and Bialla fell on 7 September. During 8 and 9 September the German 3rd Reserve Division and Goltz's Landwehr Division reputedly 'shattered' a division of the Russian XXII Corps near Arys and Bialla 'in a brilliant attack'.[15] In reality six battalions of the III and XXII corps with two artillery batteries and a Cossack detachment had been driven from Arys, with the loss of approximately 1,000 prisoners. A further twelve battalions and nine batteries of artillery failed to save Lyck during the morning of 10 September. Between 7 and 10 September the Russian XXII Finnish and III Siberian corps lost 8,000 men.

These encounters not only confused Zhilinski, but masked a good deal of administrative disarray among the Russians. Initially put under Rennenkampf, units of the embryo Tenth Army were then placed under its III Siberian Corps commander, General Radkevich, who used the staff of the Osovetz garrison pending arrival of the designated army commander, General Flug, and his staff. Quite unjustifiably, on 8 September Zhilinski told Yanushkevich at GHQ that the I and VI corps and the 3rd Guard Division of the Second Army were 'sufficiently well organised and … fully capable' of taking the offensive. Thus they should advance to the line Ortelsburg–Neidenburg to threaten the German right flank. Astonishingly, the North-West Front commander assured

Rennenkampf that the German column, which had 'come to a halt at Bialla ... turns out to be a weak one ... Consequently it represents no danger'.[16] A combination of the Russian Second and Tenth armies (the latter now being quickly reinforced as more of its units detrained) would soon clear this area and force the enemy back. Ludendorff was fully aware of this danger, fearing that his right wing 'might be overwhelmed' by the Russian 'immense superiority'.[17] Morgen and Goltz removed that anxiety. Without their success in clearing its southern flank, the Eighth Army's whole operation would have been jeopardized.

Freed from dread of a Russian assault upon its right flank, the German I Corps made rapid progress in Hindenburg's 'bold thrust' even though, following their exertions against Samsonov, Francois' men had moved 70 miles in three days. Rennenkampf's request for the XXII Corps, the right-hand formation of Tenth Army (which had been mauled by then), to return to his control had been denied by Zhilinski. So there was a generous degree of administrative confusion when Francois attacked the junction between that corps and the II Corps of the Russian First Army. The German I Corps commander enjoyed a local superiority of 4:1 as he swept the Russians aside. By the evening of 8 September Francois was well into his envelopment of Rennenkampf's left flank. The Tenth Army's I Turkestan Corps assembling in the Augustow/Osowiec area thus had no opportunity to join the battle. By his swift action Francois had bypassed it.[18]

Despite the German I Corps' success, the right wing of the Eighth Army faltered at the Lötzen Gap on 8 September. Till then the infantry of the Russian II Corps had seen little action and they now gave a good account of themselves to check the German XVII Corps. Throughout the day fierce fighting took place as Mackensen strove to break through and keep pace with Francois. Recognizing the critical nature of these tactical exchanges, Rennenkampf committed his only reserves. It was a gambler's throw, which ultimately lost. Ludendorff ordered Francois to move sharply north to hit the southern flank of the II Corps as Mackensen continued to engage its front. The sparse Russian reinforcements made scant impression.

Meanwhile, further north the main German body had advanced steadily through the Insterburg Gap, only to run into determined counter-attacks on 9 September; the decisive day. Hindenburg feared that Rennenkampf would commit his reserves here. Zhilinski was ill and, grasping the danger of Francois' rapid advance, Zhilinski's Chief of Staff advised Rennenkampf to shorten his line and concentrate on denying the Germans passage through the defiles of the Masurian Lakes. Once more the First Army commander refused to retire, fearing an adverse effect on Russian morale – and paid the price. When he realized that the Germans aimed to roll up his left flank, Rennenkampf at last withdrew the XX Corps from his right and sent it to Darkehmen to protect Gumbinnen; too late. During 9 September the German central corps regathered momentum after their temporary stutter. Meanwhile, boosted by the I Corps' assault on the flank of the Russian II Corps, Mackensen's XVII Corps had combined with it to break through the Lötzen Gap. By nightfall the two German enveloping corps were advancing rapidly towards the critical road and rail centre of Vilkovishki (east of the frontier), threatening to cut off Rennenkampf's main force.

**Battle of Masurian Lakes, 8–13 September**

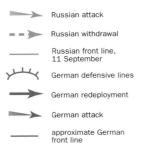

Russian attack

Russian withdrawal

Russian front line, 11 September

German defensive lines

German redeployment

German attack

approximate German front line

Further north, as the speed of the German advance caused units of the two sides to become entangled, the Russian infantry showed stubborn resistance in the many hand-to-hand encounters which developed. However, a determined counter-attack by the two divisions of IV Corps, swinging north against the German centre, did temporarily check the Eighth Army's advance. Ludendorff admitted that 'these movements did not turn out quite as I had hoped'.[19] In the chaos German units fired on one another, and others incautiously advanced without securing flank support, to their cost. Recognizing his perilous situation, Rennenkampf issued orders for a general withdrawal during the night of 9–10 September to 30 miles east of Gumbinnen. But any chance of shortening his line successfully had gone twenty-four hours before. Zhilinski's Chief of Staff had been right. Further to disrupt Rennenkampf's

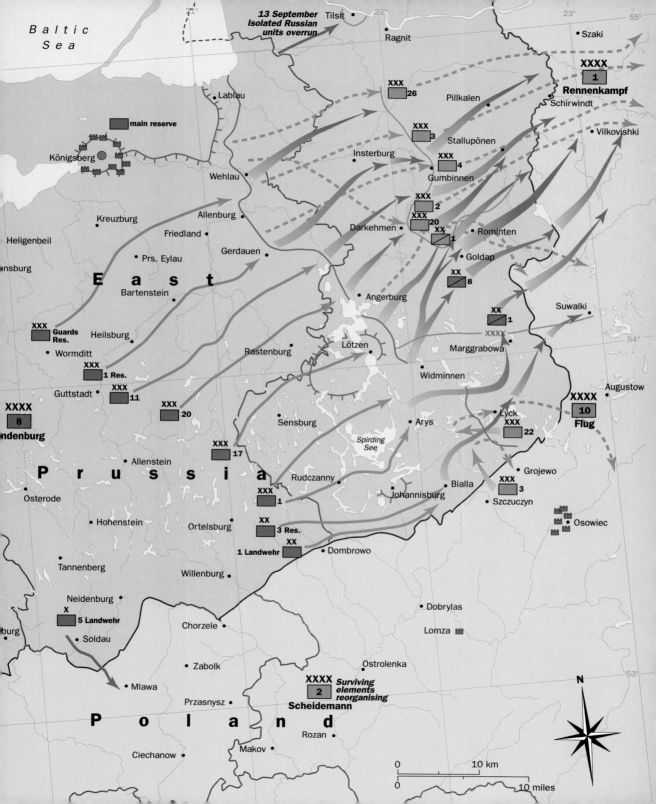

**Baltic Sea**

13 September
Isolated Russian
units overrun

Tilsit

Ragnit

Szaki

Lablau

main reserve

XXX
26

Pillkalen

XXXX
1
Rennenkampf

Schirwindt

Königsberg

XXX
3

Stallupönen

Vilkovishki

Wehlau

Insterburg

XXX
4

Gumbinnen

Kreuzburg

Allenburg

Friedland

Gerdauen

XXX
2

XXX
20

XX
1

Rominten

E  a  s  t

Prs. Eylau

Bartenstein

Darkehmen

Goldap

XX
8

Heligenbeil

nsburg

XXX
Guards
Res.

Heilsburg

Wormditt

Angerburg

XX
1

XXXX

Suwalki

Lötzen

Marggrabowa

54°

XXX
1 Res.

Guttstadt

XXX
11

Rastenburg

Widminnen

Augustow

XXXX
8

ndenburg

XXX
20

Sensburg

Spirding
See

Arys

Lyck

XXX
22

XXXX
10
Flug

P  r  u  s  s  i  a

Allenstein

XXX
17

Rudczanny

Grojewo

Osterode

Bialla

XXX
3

Szczuczyn

Hohenstein

XXX
1

Johannisburg

Osowiec

Ortelsburg

XX
3 Res.

XX
1 Landwehr

Dombrowo

Tannenberg

Willenburg

Dobrylas

Neidenburg

X
5 Landwehr

Lomza

burg

Soldau

Chorzele

N

Mlawa

Zabolk

Ostrolenka

53°

XXXX
2
Scheidemann

*Surviving
elements
reorganising*

P  o  l  a  n  d

Przasnysz

Rozan

Ciechanow

Makov

0      10 km

0      10 miles

belated plan, the order to subordinate commanders arrived at different times. So the withdrawal on 10 September from the prepared position around Gerdauen became very disjointed, with the Germans able to exploit numerous gaps between formations. However, the night retreat had been conducted so efficiently that the Germans only became aware of it when trenches near Gerdauen were found empty the following morning, and aerial reconnaissance confirmed that 'the principal Russian positions were only feebly occupied or not occupied at all'. By midday on 10 September the full extent of the Russian evacuation could be discerned. Hindenburg drew an unpalatable conclusion from this turn of events, signalling GHQ: 'It seems to me questionable whether Rennenkampf can be decisively beaten as the Russians have begun to retreat early this morning'. Hoffmann agreed that the Germans had been deprived of 'completely defeating Rennenkampf … [and] that news of his retreat was not very agreeable to us'. However, he did admit that 'the frontal attack on the admirably planned positions of the Russians would have been very difficult'. 'It appears to me doubtful if we should have been successful', he added.[20]

## THE PURSUIT

A vigorous pursuit of the Russians was set for 5 a.m. on 11 September. However, a 'most serious difficulty' developed during that day, when the XI Corps reported being attacked by a vastly superior force. Although indications from intercepted wireless messages suggested to the Eighth Army HQ that only three regiments of a Russian reserve division were involved, the XI Corps insisted on the accuracy of its own estimate. Ludendorff therefore feared that the whole central advance might be in imminent danger, with the Russians on the brink of a critical breakthrough. So he ordered the XVII and I corps to swing further north than intended. '… at least half a day' was lost before the alarming report proved unfounded. Hoffmann criticized this 'quite unnecessary stoppage in the pursuit', which went ahead despite 'the strong insistence of the Army Command [that] this loss of time could not be made up'.

Unfortunately, in Hoffmann's words 'the Chief Command allowed itself to be misled', coded inference that Hindenburg and Ludendorff and not their staff officers were to blame.[21] Specifically Hindenburg observed that a Russian concentration near Stallupönen, despite 'brilliant … feats of several of our units engaged in the pursuit' escaped 'by the skin of its teeth'. In a sense the Battle of the Masurian Lakes thus reached a tame conclusion. The Russian First Army, though heavily depleted, lived to fight another day. Ludendorff paid tribute to the effectiveness of the Russian withdrawal, which was carried out mainly at night through forested area away from main roads: 'Our airmen did certainly note the course of some retreating columns, but their reports were too vague'.[22] Hindenburg independently elaborated by explaining that, when Russian troops were caught in the open near Eydtkuhnen, German artillery blew huge gaps in their massed ranks, but 'the herding instinct filled them up again'. He reaffirmed, too, that determined rearguard action slowed 'our exhausted troops'. The Eighth Army commander declared 11 September 'a day of bloody fighting', stressing yet once more that German troops met with strong resistance as the Russian First Army withdrew.[23] That day, news of Austrian reverses in Galicia re-emphasized the need to send urgent military aid to Germany's ally, but also underlined the folly of attempting to pursue Rennenkampf beyond the Niemen. Nonetheless, the Russian First Army must still be so weakened that it could not menace the weak residue of the German Eighth Army, which would remain in East Prussia once its main units subsequently moved south into Poland.

**Russian cavalry on their way to the front.** Few mounted units involved in the 1914 East Prussian campaign distinguished themselves.

Fearing that the First Army would be totally outflanked and possibly annihilated like Samsonov's Second Army, at 5.30 p.m. on 12 September Rennenkampf ordered a continued retreat to the Niemen and moved his HQ to Kovno. That day the Russian cavalry did not distinguish itself. Nahichevanski fell back on Kunigishki; Lieutenant General Raukh's 2nd Guard Cavalry Division to Verjbolow, which left a gap for the German 8th Cavalry Division to attack the First Army's rear transport columns (Gurko's

division already having been transferred to the Tenth Army by Zhilinski). Between 6 and 9 a.m., after moving through the night, the Russian XXVI, III and IV corps recrossed the East Prussian border, by evening concentrating respectively in the Vladislvov, Vilkovishki and Budeziory–Geistorishki areas. The XX and II corps followed in their wake. During 13 September the Russian cavalry did rally to provide some cover against their German counterparts. On the extreme right of the Russian line, yet another example of inadequate communication and leadership surfaced. An isolated detachment of infantry, artillery and cavalry, sent to Tilsit on 8 September and since forgotten, was overrun.

Cornet Littauer wrote a depressing postscript for the Russian 1st Cavalry Division, which had invaded East Prussia with such high hopes on 16 August. Having briefly seen action with the Tenth Army, to which it had been belatedly transferred, Gurko's command was ordered to withdraw and Littuaer found himself in the covering rearguard. Close to Marggrabowa, where the division had mounted its first serious attack during the campaign almost a month before, Littauer had the task of destroying a crucial bridge to hamper the pursuing German troops: 'I was sorry that I have not been a better student. I looked at the bridge in dismay. I did not have any idea where to attach my charge'. Predictably his puny effort succeeded only in blowing a shower of splinters into the air, and he was extremely fortunate to gallop free as the German infantry crossed unhindered. Over the border the next day and leaving behind the efficient Prussian road system, a hussar was heard to murmur: 'In Russia, hard roads are sandy'.[24]

On the German side, during 13 September when Ludendorff decreed the battle effectively over, Mülmann's troops were moving on Mlawa; Goltz's Landwehr Division was held up outside Osowiec; the 3rd Reserve Division had taken Augustow and was approaching Suwalki; the two cavalry divisions and the I Corps were closing on Mariampol; the XVII, XX, XI and I Reserve corps stood on the line Vishtinets–Wirballen–Vladislvov; the Königsberg Main Reserve had reached Tilsit; the Guards Reserve Corps been withdrawn to

Wehlau. In the north the Russian First Army was not left quietly to lick its wounds; German infantry and cavalry continued to harass the retreating columns. Not until 15 September did the Russians claim that all the unit commanders had regained control of their scattered groups of men. At length, during the night of 18–19 September, the Russian First Army crossed the Niemen river to safety. By then, though, the battle had effectively long been over and events in the broader military and political sphere had moved on.

## DECISIVE OUTCOME

At the Masurian Lakes the Russians admitted 125,000 casualties (including 45,000 prisoners) and loss of 150 guns. With official Russian casualty figures of 3,000 and 17,000 at Stallupönen and Gumbinnen respectively during the opening phase of the campaign, the Russian First Army therefore had 145,000 casualties overall; a figure explained by reinforcements and new formations, such as the XXVI Corps. Nonetheless, Rennenkampf's army had some 100,000 survivors, a formidable force whatever their state of morale. Even before the last vestige of German pursuit had dwindled, the repercussions of defeat had begun to rumble through the Russian ranks. Recovering from his temporary illness, Zhilinski set about saving his career against charges that he had been consistently out of touch and ineffective. He contacted the different corps commanders and complained to Russian GHQ that Rennenkampf had completely lost control during the Battle of the Masurian Lakes: 'the behaviour of the Army Commander has made direction of operations impossible'. On 13 September, though, the Russian Army Chief of Staff (Yanushkevich) found Rennenkampf 'just as usual', and he kept his post. The North-West Front commander was less fortunate. Grand Duke Nikolai informed the tsar: 'I am inclined to think that General Zhilinski lost his head and in general is not capable of controlling operations'. On 17 September he was replaced by 60-year-old General Nikolai Ruzski.[25]

Ludendorff did not have long to savour the Eighth Army's triumph. While celebrating at Insterburg on 14 September, he learned of his appointment to an identical post with the army being formed by General von Schubert at Breslau. The next morning he took his leave of Hindenburg and set off by car. Dining at Allenstein, he remarked that 'life had already resumed its old course as in times of peace';[26] an oblique tribute to the Eighth Army's achievements.

Meanwhile, Grand Duke Nikolai had issued fresh orders to the First, Second and Tenth armies to regroup and stabilize the front along the Niemen river. He thus acknowledged that the invasion of East Prussia had been an abject failure.

# EPILOGUE: COUNTING THE COST

The two and a half weeks between 26 August and 13 September 1914 undoubt-edly witnessed a major Russian military disaster. The Germans incurred an estimated 37,000 casualties. The North-West Front suffered some 250,000 casualties (killed, wounded and prisoners), quite apart from the loss of enor-mous amounts of equipment and guns. One army commander committed suicide, three corps commanders became prisoners. The attempt to defeat the German Eighth Army and occupy East Prussia failed abysmally, despite a supe-riority in numbers of roughly 2:1. The short-term effects were undisputed. The wider significance and long-term impact were less easy to determine; explaining the catastrophe inescapably contentious.

## RUSSIAN COMMANDERS

Based on reports that they had physically exchanged blows a decade before over failure to come to one another's aid during the Russo-Japanese War, crit-icism has been widely levelled at the choice of Rennenkampf and Samsonov to lead the two armies involved in East Prussia. The corollary maintains that their antagonism resulted in deliberate non-cooperation and the ultimate military debacle. Hoffmann, the German Eighth Army staff officer, recalled that during the campaign he spoke to Ludendorff about 'the feud between the two enemy leaders' and their enduring 'personal enmity'[1] However, there is no convincing evidence that either general deliberately failed to support the other. Both undoubtedly evaded or ignored instructions from Zhilinski, but not for reasons demonstrably linked to their alleged personal antipathy.

**Defeat.** A Russian strongpoint overrun during the battle of the Masurian Lakes in September 1914. Note the dead soldiers (foreground).

Furthermore the oft repeated story of their unseemly bout of fisticuffs on Mukden station may well be mythical, Rennenkampf having in reality clashed with another officer named Mishchenko.

The professional performances of both army commanders in the field may be more open to question; one striking feature of the East Prussian campaign being lack of comprehensive cavalry reconnaissance. Pre-invasion forays over the border were haphazard, and neither general probed effectively ahead of his infantry once on German soil. The Russian military doctrine assumed that corps commanders would use their own attached cavalry for this purpose. However, due to the cumbersome mobilization process and accelerated speed of advance, few of these second- and third-line units had arrived before battle was joined. Single squadrons detached from the main cavalry formations proved totally inadequate substitutes. Samsonov's failure to take more positive steps to determine the full deployment of his German opponents before launching the Second Army's attack across the southern frontier is clearly debatable. If he had done so, he might not have weakened his line by extending it so far west. The British writer Major General Sir Edmund Ironside has pointed out that, if the II Corps east of the Masurian Lakes were included, Samsonov's five and a half corps and three cavalry divisions sprawled 135 miles east to west. Rennenkampf's failings before and after the opening clashes at Stallupönen and Gumbinnen, his inability to detect the southward transfer of German forces to attack Samsonov and his similar shortcomings before the Battle of the Masurian Lakes may also be questioned. Possibly he and Samsonov were affected by their experiences during the Russo-Japanese War, when several cavalry sorties were mauled by Japanese infantry. Brigadier General Knox believed that the career of neither army commander fitted him 'to contend with men who had made a lifelong study of war in this [European] theatre and under the existing conditions'. Still puzzled by the Russian commander's curious inactivity in East Prussia, Hindenburg reflected after the war that either Rennenkampf's reputation had been unreasonably inflated or he had 'lost his military qualities' since the Russo-Japanese War.[2] Nonetheless, attempts to focus blame for the debacle on the two army commanders alone lacks persuasion.

Whether or not Rennenkampf and Samsonov were culpable, they were not well served by their subordinate commanders. In the Second Army, Artamonov (I Corps) was replaced; Blagoveshchenski (VI Corps) proved indecisive; Kondratovich (XXIII Corps) ineffective; Klyuev (XIII Corps) seemed hesitant when unexpected problems arose. None of the First Army's corps commanders distinguished themselves; particularly Nahichevanski (Cavalry

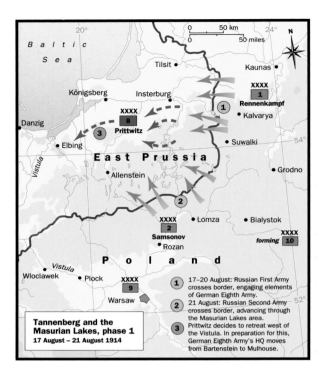

**Tannenberg and the Masurian Lakes, phase 1**
**17 August – 21 August 1914**

1  17–20 August: Russian First Army crosses border, engaging elements of German Eighth Army.

2  21 August: Russian Second Army crosses border, advancing through the Masurian Lakes area.

3  Prittwitz decides to retreat west of the Vistula. In preparation for this, German Eighth Army's HQ moves from Bartenstein to Mulhouse.

**Phase 2**
**21–26 August 1914**

4  Russian forces slowly advance into East Prussia.

5  Hindenburg replaces Prittwitz. Hindenburg changes the German plan moving the bulk of the Eighth Army to face the Russian Second Army leaving a Cavalry screen facing the Russian First Army.

Corps) and Oranovski (1st Independent Cavalry Brigade). Rennenkampf may be criticized for not getting rid of Nahichevanski, whom he clearly distrusted; Samsonov sacked Artamonov. Nahichevanski may have been saved by his influential cavalry contacts. Official enquiries later acquitted the I Corps commander, but dismissed from the service Blagoveschenski, Kondratovich and Lieutenant General Komarov, commander of the 4th Infantry Division; Knox noted that military opinion unofficially blamed Klyuev for surrendering his corps prematurely.

There was no excuse for Zhilinski, who had been closely concerned with the entire concept of attacking Germany in support of France and the detailed plans to fulfil Russia's political commitment in this respect. He had played the part of the North-West Front commander during the Kiev war games. Yet once

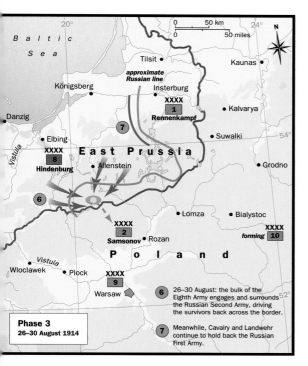

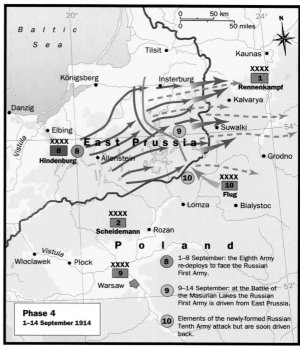

**Phase 3**
**26–30 August 1914**

(6) 26–30 August: the bulk of the Eighth Army engages and surrounds the Russian Second Army, driving the survivors back across the border.

(7) Meanwhile, Cavalry and Landwehr continue to hold back the Russian First Army.

**Phase 4**
**1–14 September 1914**

(8) 1–8 September: the Eighth Army re-deploys to face the Russian First Army.

(9) 9–14 September: at the Battle of the Masurian Lakes the Russian First Army is driven from East Prussia.

(10) Elements of the newly-formed Russian Tenth Army attack but are soon driven back.

hostilities commenced, he failed abysmally in terms of leadership, strategy and man-management; 'a model of ineptitude' in Norman Stone's opinion.[3] Quite unjustifiably, for example, he assured GHQ that both his armies would be ready by 11 August, and he made no effort to verify the optimistic reports from either army. Personally he did not stir from the North-West Front HQ. He based his subsequent orders to the First Army on Rennenkampf's contention that the Germans had been decisively beaten at Gumbinnen. Evidently he did not query how an enemy routed by Rennenkampf could have attacked the Second Army so strongly. He cajoled, but failed to act positively, when Samsonov simply bypassed his orders and unwisely extended the Second Army front westwards prior to the invasion of East Prussia; nor did he goad Rennenkampf into action when Samsonov was under attack. The North-

West Front commander appeared obsessed by his own plan for the double envelopment of the German Eighth Army. Presumably on the basis that Samsonov was being attacked by the remnants of a beaten force, he seemed to expect the Second Army to triumph and thus continue northwards virtually unhindered to link with the First Army. During the battle of the Masurian Lakes, refusing to admit that the Second Army was a spent force, he still flirted with the concept of double envelopment of the German Eighth Army. He thus not only required Rennenkampf to advance south-south-west behind the Lakes, but also ordered part of the new Tenth Army to Lomza away from the First Army's vulnerable left flank. Flexibility did not figure in his vocabulary.

## RUSSIAN STAFF

Golovine held staff officers at GHQ and the North-West Front responsible for a raft of costly inefficiencies. He claimed that they grossly underestimated the firepower of German infantry divisions, which exceeded that of their Russian equivalents by some 50 per cent. 'There was not much truth in this', Stone has observed, merely a convenient post-operational apologia. The same may be said of Golovine's persistent and questionable claims that the numbers and quality of the Russian artillery were inferior to the German artillery. He was on safer ground in arguing that the effectiveness of the Landwehr formations had been fatally miscalculated. Unlike the Russian militia, these troops were well trained and ready to take their place at the front with first-line and reserve units from the outbreak of war. In East Prussia they provided an invaluable, and for the Russians unexpected, boost to the German Eighth Army. Golovine attacked the staffs at Baranovichi and Bialystok for lack of clear vision, once the initial plan for double envelopment had broken down. They undoubtedly did tend to react to developments in the field, rather than anticipate them. In fairness, though, the unexpected pace of the action, exacerbated by inadequate communications and inevitable lack of reliable information, often obscured the true military situation. With the benefit of hindsight, Golovine made no allowance for these drawbacks. 'The General Staff ... were zealous in diffusing inaccurate information',[4] he sharply concluded. He may well be right. Furthermore, the choice of double envelopment, rather than concentration of the numerically superior Russian forces against the one army defending East Prussia, appears with hindsight a monumental strategic error. For this staff officers at the highest level must be accountable. By August 1914 those who implemented the plans had no choice.

In their partial defence, the staffs were hamstrung by the tight timetable forced upon them. The political commitment to France and subsequent military undertakings were responsible, in Golovine's view 'literally <u>fatal</u> ... the chief reason for the sad issue of Russia of the whole war'. The Russian critic went on to identify the perpetrators of these follies as the real villains and the promise of operations on the fifteenth day of mobilization as unforgivable. As a result, in East Prussia the First and Second armies were required to carry out 'operations of a quite fantastic character'. The Germans were expected to have first-line reinforcement in East Prussia five days after their general mobilization. So the Russians must invade in strength at least a day earlier – utterly impossible. 'The history of the campaign of 1914 is nothing else but the story of the consequences of the strategical errors of the War Plan', he concluded not unreasonably. Bismarck would have cast the net wider. No nation 'should sacrifice its existence on the altar of fidelity to a treaty' he once argued. Realpolitik, not conscience, was the stuff of statesmanship in his view.[5]

The sloppy use of wireless and telephonic communications by the Russians, which presented the Germans with crucial intelligence, has been widely condemned as a prime example of near-criminal incompetence. Quoting an immediate post-war Russian source, N.V. Abakanovich, Norman Stone has pointed out that Samsonov's army had twenty-five telephones, very few Morse coding machines, and a single primitive and slow teleprinter which frequently broke down. Most of the wireless operators were undertrained and thus unable to cope with encoding procedures; GHQ at Baranovichi had a single Morse coding apparatus, which only six men were qualified to use. The shortcomings therefore were the fault more of an arthritic communications system than of hard-pressed operators in the field. Adequate, reliable means were simply not at their disposal. It is worth noting that Ludendorff often complained of the sparse means of communication, especially telephones, available to the Germans in East Prussia.

## SIGNIFICANCE OF THE MARNE

Whether or not the diversion of two German corps and a cavalry division from the Western Front led to successful French resistance at the Battle of the Marne (5–9 September) is perhaps the fundamental issue surrounding the entire East Prussian campaign. Lieutenant Colonel Tappen, Chief of Operations at GHQ, believed that German progress in the west coupled with news of the advance of two Russian armies into East Prussia persuaded Moltke that he could spare these units to save the province and remove an immediate threat to Berlin. When Prittwitz sent such depressing situation reports in the third week of August, five German armies involved in the wheel through Belgium and northern France were making rapid progress, and Moltke thought that he could afford to reinforce East Prussia. Hoffmann, who was with Ludendorff when he received two relevant phone calls from Tappen during the closing stages of the Battle of Tannenberg, confirmed that the initiative for the redeployment came entirely from Koblenz. Later Tappen wrote: 'I admit that this was a mistake which had its revenge upon us at the Marne'. In retrospect Marshal Ferdinand Foch insisted that East Prussia 'eased the task of the French and British armies at the Battle of the Marne … [making] an appreciable reduction of forces facing the Allies'. Ludendorff held that 'the withdrawal of the Guards Reserve Corps and XI Corps … made itself felt with fatal results'.[6] Even if the Battle of the Marne were invested with the pivotal importance so widely ascribed to it, arguably its outcome rested on a series of German tactical mistakes rather than lack of four infantry divisions and one cavalry division. As the extreme right wing, from west to east Kluck's First and Bülow's Second armies, approached the apogee of the Schlieffen Plan, on 27 August Moltke liberated Kluck from Bülow's overall command. Then, on 2 September, he ordered Kluck to march east of Paris to cover Bülow's right flank as both armies pursued south-eastwards the retreating British Expeditionary Force (BEF) and French Fifth Army. After the war, to Major General J.E.B. Seely (the peacetime British politician and in 1914 liaison officer at Field Marshal Sir John French's BEF Headquarters), Kluck reflected: 'If I had a blind eye and a deaf ear like your Lord Nelson, I should not now be sitting, entertaining you in this humble lodging as a soldier of a defeated army'.[7]

Kluck had a selective memory. When the order arrived, he was one day's march ahead of Bülow. Exercising his independence and believing that he alone could catch the enemy, Kluck did not wait for the Second Army and 'echelon' to the right rear behind it as required, but pressed ahead. Kluck seemed unaware of a serious threat to his right flank and rear, but to comply with Moltke's order he would need to pause for up to thirty-six hours for Bülow to catch up and pass him. His appreciation of the military situation deemed that most unwise, as it would allow the French Fifth Army and BEF to reorganize ahead of his pursuing army. Captain B.H. Liddell Hart, the British commentator, has argued that Moltke asked Kluck impossibly to 'perform a sort of backward somersault'.[8]

Nonetheless, by his action Kluck exposed his right flank to attack from the French Sixth Army and the 8th Division of the Fourth Army, which soon arrived in the line to its immediate right (half of the newcomers being dramatically transported to the front in the legendary Paris taxicabs). Kluck had put his two left-hand corps (the III and IX Reserve) temporarily under Bülow, so close contact between the two German armies was being maintained. However, when the French began seriously to embarrass his own right flank, during the evening of 6 September Kluck recalled the detached corps. He left only a weak force of cavalry and light infantry to plug a 30 mile gap between

**General Alexander von Kluck (1846–1934).** Kluck commanded the German First Army on the extreme right of the sweep through Belgium in August 1914 during execution of the Schlieffen Plan. He fatally allowed a gap to open up with the Second Army east of Paris, which led to defeat in the first battle of the Marne.

the two armies, which the Allies would ultimately exploit. Whether the troops sent to East Prussia could have favourably redressed this perilous development is the crucial question. Only the Guards Reserve Corps belonged to the German Second Army; the XI Corps came from the Third Army to its left. As the conflict progressed, Bülow's manoeuvres were not dictated by absence of his corps. After Kluck recalled his two corps on 6 September, a further complication arose. In articulating his orders for carrying the frontier fortresses and encircling Verdun, on 4 September Moltke had ordered both armies of the extreme German right wing to face westwards as flank cover. To achieve this, Bülow pulled back his right to the right bank of the Petit Morin river, so widening the gap with the First Army still more. Coupled with Kluck's withdrawal of his corps from here to his right (northern) flank, this movement persuaded the BEF that the Germans were in retreat.

At 9 a.m. on 9 September, Bülow received aerial reconnaissance reports that

**Transport under fire.** A British Expeditionary Force transport column under shell fire during the first battle of the Marne. The soldier (centre) belongs to the Intelligence Corps and has been wounded in the face by shrapnel.

# Le Petit Journal

ADMINISTRATION
61, RUE LAFAYETTE, 61

Les manuscrits ne sont pas rendus

On s'abonne sans frais
dans tous les bureaux de poste

5 CENT.

**SUPPLÉMENT ILLUSTRÉ**

5 CENT.

26ᵐᵉ Année

Numéro 1.289

ABONNEMENTS

SEINE et SEINE-ET-OISE .. 2 fr.    5 fr. 50
DÉPARTEMENTS............. 2 fr.    4 fr. »
ÉTRANGER................. 2 50    5 fr. »

DIMANCHE 5 SEPTEMBRE 1915

## UN GRAND ANNIVERSAIRE
### 5 au 12 septembre 1914 — La victoire de la Marne

**Victory.** A dramatic illustration celebrating the French triumph during the first battle of the Marne in September 1914.

six Allied columns (mainly BEF) had been spotted marching north towards the crucial gap. Two hours later, fearful of being outflanked, Bülow issued a unilateral order to retreat (later supported in person by Lieutenant Colonel Richard Hensch, Head of Foreign Armies (Intelligence) at GHQ). So at 2 p.m. the German Second Army began to fall back. Aiming to straighten the whole German line, following the latest check on the eastern frontier of France, during that evening of 8 September Hensch had ordered Kluck to retreat to Soissons. On 9 September, as the German Second Army thus withdrew north-eastwards, the First Army went north to widen the gap to 30 miles. Under the circumstances it is difficult to see how the loss to the Eighth Army of the two corps (only one from the Second Army) could have altered a situation which had evolved through a catalogue of German strategic and tactical decisions by individual commanders, none swayed by loss of the absent divisions. Before events on the Marne, the German offensive had already run out of steam; lack of a breakthrough from Lorraine and inability to reinforce the right wing were the factors which led to the withdrawal of Kluck and Bülow.

The conclusions of Foch and Moltke, for example, should be judged in this light. Moltke metaphorically wrung his hands and ascribed failure of the opening phase of the war to a reverse at the Marne and dispatch of the two corps to East Prussia. In reality his own earlier planning and strategic miscalculations, not least in launching and persisting with assaults on the frontier fortresses, determined failure. Perhaps sensitive to France's part in coaxing Russia into the disastrous East Prussian venture and mindful of her post-war anti-Bolshevik stance, writing over a decade later Foch therefore highlighted transfer of the two corps to the east for political reasons. There was, too, attempted justification of the monumental reverses in East Prussia from ex-tsarist officers like Golovine, who underlined the allegedly decisive action on the Marne; Russia's indirect contribution to Allied success; her integrity in adhering to treaty obligations and staff undertakings.

**Post-operational briefing.** Hindenburg (left) explains to Kaiser Wilhelm II how the Russians were beaten during the battle of Tannenberg, as Ludendorff (right) looks on.

## LUCK

Events in East Prussia during August and September 1914 underlined Napoleon's dictum on the need for luck in warfare. Hindenburg and Ludendorff emerged from those months as national heroes. If Prittwitz had held his nerve on 20 August, not made his fateful telephone call to Moltke announcing the intention of retreating to the Vistula, or had made a second call telling the C-in-C that he had reversed that decision, Hindenburg would not have been summoned from retirement nor Ludendorff been sent to the east. Thus they could not have burnished their military reputations at Russian expense. Before they arrived Hoffmann had already drawn up plans to defeat Samsonov before Rennenkampf, hence there was no need for the new arrivals to convince the Eighth Army Staff about the wisdom of redeployment. Moreover, orders had already been issued and relevant movements commenced before Hindenburg and Ludendorff reached Marienburg on 23 August. They were fortunate to encounter no resistance to such a bold initiative from staff officers, already attuned to its implications, and benefited from the fact that troops had already begun to entrain for the south. Napoleon's slice of luck.

Writing his account of the East Prussian campaign in 1926 and without claiming to have originated the decisive movements himself, Hoffmann deplored the enduring myth that Hindenburg had been primarily responsible for planning the destruction of Samsonov's army; nor did he specifically mention Ludendorff in this context. Alluding to the lengthy pre-war discussions surrounding implementation of the Schlieffen Plan, he firmly declared that 'Tannenberg is not the work of a single man'. In an acid letter to Hoffmann in 1925, Francois wrote that 'the part played by Ludendorff at Tannenberg was not such, in my opinion, that he can claim any credit for its success'. He went on swingeingly to declare that 'Ludendorff's recollections have no historical value'. In the same letter, Francois asserted that only by ignoring Ludendorff's unreasonable orders did he secure success on the Russian left flank; another example of retrospective ego polishing. Hoffmann, however, had no doubts about Ludendorff, '... a fine fellow to work with. He is the right man for the business – ruthless and hard'.[9]

## LOGISTICS

Logistics provided the key to German success in East Prussia. The poor Russian infrastructure (inadequate roads and railways, which drastically slowed progress south of the frontier), the sparse and insecure wireless communications in battle, the woeful supply and reinforcement system (exacerbated by a cumbersome mobilization process) undoubtedly proved serious handicaps to the invaders. The Germans enjoyed the ability to operate on interior lines and the existence of a comprehensive rail network, much of it with double-track lines and all of it incapable of being used by Russian rolling stock created for a different gauge. But these advantages had to be exploited, and this the Germans did admirably. Furthermore, Russian airmen in the combat zone were severely handicapped by lack of petrol.

## MECHANIZATION

With the dawn of mechanization reconnaissance no longer rested wholly with the cavalry, and the performance of the fourth arm of warfare, the air services, remains enigmatic. Many reconnaissance flights were flown, both by the Russians and by the Germans. Given the wide areas to be covered, aerial reconnaissance made theoretical sense, and there were undoubtedly isolated successes on both sides. However, the flimsy, low-flying machines were vulnerable to small arms fire, and few commanders yet placed their trust in the air. So aircraft (aeroplanes and airships) did not play a central role in East Prussia, not least because in August and September 1914 their flying personnel were experiencing a European baptism of fire. Military air services of every nation were in their infancy. Significantly, both Hindenburg and Ludendorff commented on the inadequacies of German aerial reconnaissance during the campaign. Russian lack of transport on the ground is also noteworthy. For its invasion of East Prussia, the Second Army could muster only ten cars and four defective motorcycles.

## CONCLUSIONS

The British military attaché, Brigadier General A.W.F. Knox, delivered a devastating epitaph on the campaign: 'The Russians were just great big-hearted children, who had thought out nothing and had stumbled half-asleep into a wasp's nest'. In another sweeping conclusion, the American commentator Major General Stuart Heintzelman has written that the campaign showed 'the dire results of faulty preliminary plans for supply, maintenance, and communication, and for the necessity for the dominant assertion of their authority by the higher leaders'. Neither Heintzelman nor Knox were unreasonable. The overwhelming impression of a flawed military plan, incompetently carried out and launched primarily to meet treaty obligations, is inescapable. The irony may well be that military action in East Prussia and the premature launching of Plan A had no real impact on the Western Front. Conversely, it did adversely affect public support in Russia and undermine Allied confidence in the military capability of the tsar's army.[10]

For the Germans the campaign in East Prussia provided an opportune propaganda boost after failure to conquer France. Tsarist officers condemned to exile by the Communist revolution similarly reinvented the fate of an honourable regime undone by its political integrity, which led to fulfilment of its treaty obligations and military undertakings at all costs. Thus may the veil of myth obscure the reality of incompetence.

# CHRONOLOGY

| | |
|---|---|
| 1871 | France defeated in the Franco-Prussian War; new German Empire declared |
| 1879 | Dual Alliance: military pact between Germany and Austria-Hungary |
| 1882 | Italy joins to create the Triple Alliance, but not bound to fight Britain |
| 1891–3 | Franco-Russian political and military agreements culminate in the so-called Dual Entente |
| 1893–1913 | Franco-Russian military staff talks to determine plans for co-operation against Germany and Austria-Hungary in time of war |
| 1904 | Entente Cordiale between Britain and France |
| 1904–5 | Russo-Japanese War: Russia militarily humiliated; in peace treaty loses Port Arthur and Manchuria, recognizes Korea as Japanese sphere of influence |
| 1905–12 | Secret military staff talks between British and French officers |
| 1906 | Schlieffen Plan finalized to counteract a war on two fronts (Russia and France); France to be the priority target |
| 1907 | Russo-British agreement on colonial spheres of interest creates the basis of a Triple Entente |

## 1914

| | |
|---|---|
| 20–24 April | Russian war games in Kiev |
| 28 June | Austrian Archduke Franz Ferdinand assassinated at Sarajevo |
| 5 July | Germany pledges full support to Austria-Hungary |
| 23 July | Austro-Hungarian ultimatum to Servia |
| 24 July | Servia appeals to Russia for support |
| 25 July | Servia accepts all but one point of the Austrian ultimatum |
| | Russian partial mobilization on Austro-Hungarian border |
| 26 July | Austro-Hungarian partial mobilization on the border |
| 28 July | Austria-Hungary general mobilization, declares war on Servia |
| | Appointment of commanders to the Russian North-West Front, First and Second armies (destined for the East Prussian campaign) confirmed |
| 29 July | Austrians bombard Belgrade |
| | Belgium mobilizes |
| | Russia asks Germany to restrain Austria-Hungary |
| 30 July | Britain rejects Germany's call for her to stay neutral |
| | Nicholas II agrees to general mobilization |
| 31 July | Russian general mobilization commences; Germany threatens war, if not cancelled |
| 1 August | Germany and France announce general mobilization |
| | Germany declares war on Russia |
| 2 August | Grand Duke Nikolai Nikolaievich appointed Commander-in-Chief of the Russian armed forces |
| | Germany invades Luxembourg |
| | Germany demands passage through Belgium |
| | Italy announces neutrality |

| 3 August | Germany declares war on France |
| | Belgium rejects German demand |
| | Britain mobilizes |
| | Russian cavalry begin probes into East Prussia |

| 4 August | Germany invades Belgium; Britain declares war |

| 5 August | French ambassador formally asks the tsar to support France by attacking Germany |

| 6 August | Russia decides to invade East Prussia |
| | Austria-Hungary declares war on Russia |
| | Servia declares war on Germany |

| 10 August | Russian First and Second armies to concentrate for the invasion of East Prussia by 11 August |

| 12 August | Major Russian cavalry sweeps into East Prussia |
| | Samsonov arrives to take command of the Russian Second Army |

| 13 August | Russian North-West Front commander (Zhilinski) issues detailed orders to his First and Second armies |

| 14 August | German Eighth Army commander (Prittwitz) learns that Russian troops are on the move; issues orders 'to combat an invasion of East Prussia' |

| 15 August | Russian First Army commander (Rennenkampf) issues his orders |

| 16 August | Russian cavalry cross the East Prussian frontier ahead of the First Army |
| | Zhilinski objects to Samsonov unilaterally assuming command of the I and Guard corps, which were under North-West Front's control |

| | |
|---|---|
| 17 August | Main body of the Russian First Army crosses eastern frontier of East Prussia |
| | First main clash of the campaign: skirmish at Stallupönen, German I Corps retires under orders |
| 19 August | Zhilinski agrees to the Russian I Corps coming under Samsonov |
| 20 August | Battle of Gumbinnen: German attack held |
| | German Eighth Army commander receives news that another Russian force (Samsonov's Second Army) is approaching the southern frontier of East Prussia; orders disengagement before the First Army and retirement to the Vistula river; informs German GHQ at Coblenz; persuaded to change orders but fails to tell GHQ |
| | Russian Guard Corps comes under Samsonov |
| 20–21 August | Russian Second Army crosses the southern frontier of East Prussia, spread out and at different times |
| 21 August | German Chief of the General Staff (Moltke) decides to replace the Eighth Army commander and his Chief of Staff |
| 22 August | Assuming that the Germans have been driven back before him and in the north have been routed at Gumbinnen, Samsonov prepares to advance west of the Masurian Lakes and meet the victorious First Army to complete a decisive double envelopment of the German Eighth Army |
| | The XV Corps of the Russian Second Army bombards Neidenburg |
| | The Russian II Corps (east of the Masurian Lakes) is transferred to the First Army |
| | Hindenburg and Ludendorff appointed respectively General Officer Commanding and Chief of Staff to the German |

Eighth Army; Ludendorff issues new orders, in reality amending the revised orders of 20 August

23 August
The Russian XV Corps encounters German opposition in the Orlau/Frankenau area; held up overnight and suffers heavy casualties

Hindenburg and Ludendorff reach East Prussia

23–25 August
While a thin screen covers the fortress of Königsberg on the Baltic coast from the Russian First Army in the north, four German corps and one independent division transferred to the south prepared to attack the Russian Second Army

24 August
Russian Second Army's advance resumes, but the VI Corps on the right now separated by 30 miles from the other three and a half corps

25 August
German Eighth Army poised to attack the Russian Second Army; intercepted wireless messages confirm Samsonov's intentions and the fact that the First Army in the north would remain passive

26 August
Battle of Tannenberg opens

German I Corps takes Seeben Heights on Russian left

Russian centre advances before being held along the Drewenz river and south of Mühlen

On Russian right, VI Corps driven back from Bischofsburg by the German XVII and I Reserve corps

Message from the German GHQ at Koblenz, announcing intention to dispatch to East Prussia three additional infantry corps (two eventually sent) and one cavalry division from the Western Front

| 27 August | On the Russian left flank, Usdau falls and a counter-offensive at Heinrichsdorf fails; Russian I Corps commander (Artamonov) dismissed |
| | In the centre, the Russian XXIII Corps retreats, Neidenburg under German attack; Russian XV Corps slows the advance of the German XX Corps; Russian XIII Corps occupies Allenstein |
| | On the Russian right, the VI Corps continues to fall back |
| 28 August | The Russian Second Army Commander (Samsonov) unaware of the defeats on his right and left flanks due to poor communications |
| | Russians driven back in the centre; Samsonov hopes to rally at Neidenburg, which the Germans occupy; Russian XXIII Corps commander (Kondratovich) dismissed |
| | The Russian VI Corps rallies on the right; Germans fail to overcome |
| 29 August | The German I Corps outflanks the Russian left, patrols the road from Neidenburg to Willenburg, attempting to cut off the southern escape route |
| | Ludendorff aims to encircle the Russian XIII, XV and part of the XXIII corps in the centre; these broken formations fight their way towards the southern border |
| | Commander of the Russian XV Corps captured |
| | Hindenburg claims victory |
| 30 August | Only isolated groups of Russians evade capture |
| | 20,000 (including the XIII Corps commander Klyuev) surrender |
| | Russian counter-attack by the reorganized residue of the XXIII Corps retakes Neidenburg |

| | |
|---|---|
| 31 August | Russian Second Army commander (Samsonov) commits suicide |
| | Russians withdraw from Neidenburg; last survivors recross the southern frontier |
| | The Russian I and XXIII corps from the left and the VI Corps from the right have retained some shape; the XIII and XV corps have been annihilated. |
| | The Russian GHQ urges Rennenkampf's First Army to attack German lines of communication, knowing that the Eighth Army would now turn on it |
| | Hindenburg informed that two infantry divisions and a cavalry division are on their way to him; arrived in time for the Battle of the Masurian Lakes |
| 1 September | Rennenkampf refuses to withdraw to more secure lines or to concentrate his dispersed cavalry |
| | The Germans begin to transfer troops northwards for an attack on the Russian First Army |
| 4 September | Zhilinski (Russian North-West Front commander) believes that a German attack on Mlawa in Poland is likely; appears not to suspect an assault on Rennenkampf |
| | News that a Russian Tenth Army is gathering south of the frontier, comprising three corps |
| | German transfer of troops almost complete; Russians seemingly unaware of its extent due to inadequate ground and aerial reconnaissance |
| 5 September | Zhilinski forsees revival of the double-envelopment plan with a revitalized Second Army and new Tenth Army co-operating with the First Army |
| 5–9 September | First Battle of the Marne; the Schlieffen Plan fails |

| | |
|---|---|
| 7 September | Rennenkampf remains on the defensive, with the XX Corps on his right (northern) flank, and IV Corps the centre, II Corps and a reserve division in the south; reports that strong German forces are advancing towards him on a wide front |
| | The Germans have Landwehr troops guarding their left (northern) flank, four infantry corps (Guard Reserve, I Reserve, XI and XX) facing Rennenkampf's centre, with I and XVII corps aiming to drive northwards behind (east of) the Masurian Lakes and roll up the Russian left flank, with their own southernflank protected by the 3rd Reserve Division and the 1st Landwehr Division |
| | Zhilinski orders deployment of those parts of the three Tenth Army corps which have reached the forward area |
| | In the south-east, the German covering force takes Bialla |
| 8 September | The German I Corps sweeps rapidly round the south of the Masurian Lakes and turns north; but determined Russian opposition prevents the XVII Corps debouching from the Lötzen Gap to meet it |
| | On the right flank of the German I Corps, the 3rd Reserve Division and the 1st Landwehr Division continue to advance; Zhilinski wrongly informs GHQ that they have been halted and the Russian Second Army is ready to resume the offensive |
| | The four German corps advance in the centre and north |
| 9 September | The German XVII Corps breaks out of the Lötzen Gap and with the I Corps, supported by two cavalry divisions, turns the Russian left flank |
| | Rennenkampf withdraws his right flank eastwards to stronger positions, as the Germans are counter-attacked by the Russian IV Corps in the centre |

Rennenkampf recognizes his perilous position and in the evening orders a general retreat through forested areas during the night

| | |
|---|---|
| 10 September | The Germans find strong Russian defences abandoned |
| 11 September | A vigorous pursuit mounted by the Germans during which the XI Corps falsely reports a dangerous counter-attack; the I and XVII corps are ordered to alter direction north-westwards to deal with this perceived threat; resultant delay to the southern outflanking movement allows many Russians to escape the closing net |
| | Russian rearguard fights valiantly, as the main force recrosses the frontier; Hindenburg complains of vague, unhelpful aerial reconnaissance reports |
| 12 September | Fearing encirclement, Rennenkampf orders retirement to the Niemen river, 50 miles inside Russia |
| 13 September | An isolated Russian detachment near Tilsit overrun German troops and move forward into Russia along the whole line, but meet resistance |
| | Battle effectively over; East Prussia cleared of Russian troops Hindenburg ordered to send units south to fight the Austrians; resists but the focus of attention has now shifted from East Prussia |
| 15 September | Ludendorff leaves the Eighth Army for a similar post at Breslau |
| 17 September | Zhilinski removed from command |
| 19 September | Russians recross the Niemen; pursuit finally called off. |

# APPENDIX A

**BATTLES OF TANNENBERG AND THE MASURIAN LAKES**

**AUGUST–SEPTEMBER 1914**

## GERMAN ORDER OF BATTLE

### EIGHTH ARMY

| | |
|---|---|
| General Officer Commanding | Colonel General Max von Prittwitz und Gaffron (from 23 August  Colonel General Paul Ludwig Hans Anton von Beneckendorff und von Hindenburg) |
| Chief of Staff | Major General Count von Waldersee (from 23 August  Major General Erich Ludendorff) |

**Infantry Formations**

| | |
|---|---|
| I Corps | General of Infantry von Francois |
| 1st Division | Lieutenant General von Conta |
| 2nd Division | Lieutenant General von Falk |
| | |
| XVII Corps | General of Cavalry von Mackensen |
| 35th Division | Lieutenant General Hennig |
| 36th Division | Lieutenant General von Heineccius |
| | |
| XX Corps | General of Artillery von Scholtz |
| 37th Division | Lieutenant General von Staabs |
| 41st Division | Major General Sontag |

| I Reserve Corps | Lieutenant General von Below |
| 1st Reserve Division | Lieutenant General von Förster |
| 36th Reserve Division | Major General Kruge |

| XI Corps* | General of Infantry von Plüskow |
| 22nd Division | Major General Dieffenbach |
| 38th Division | Lieutenant General Wagner |

| Guards Reserve Corps* | General of Artillery von Gallwitz |
| 3rd Guard Division | Lieutenant General von Bonin |
| 1st Guard Reserve Division | Major General Albrecht |

\* arrived from the Western Front in time for the Battle of the Masurian Lakes

| 3rd Reserve Division | Lieutenant General von Morgen |
| | (independent command) |

## Cavalry formations

| 1st Cavalry Division | Lieutenant General Brecht |
| 8th Cavalry Division† | Major General Count von der Schulenburg |

† arrived from the Western Front in time for the Battle of the Masurian Lakes

## Landwehr formations

| 1st Landwehr Division* | Lieutenant General Baron von der Goltz |

\* arrived from Schleswig-Holstein on 27 August

| 2nd  Landwehr Brigade | Colonel Baron von Lupin |
| 6th Landwehr Brigade | Major General Krahmer |
| 70th Landwehr Brigade | Major General Breithaupt |

## Garrison troops in the field

| Danzig | fortress detachment (returned to Danzig, 21 August) |
| Königsberg Main Reserve | one composite division: Lieutenant General Brodrück |

| | |
|---|---|
| Kulm, Graudenz and Marienburg | one composite brigade: Major General von Unger |
| Posen Main Reserve: | Major General Count von Bredow |
| 19th Landwehr Brigade | Major General von Schauroth |
| | |
| Thorn  Main Reserve (35th Reserve Division) | Lieutenant General von Schmettau |
| 5th Landwehr Brigade | Lieutenant General von Mülmann |
| 20th Landwehr Brigade | Lieutenant General von Hertzberg |

Not included are an unknown number of Landsturm units, the static Königsberg and Lötzen garrisons and the equivalent of a composite brigade guarding the lines of communication.

## RUSSIAN ORDER OF BATTLE

(not every divisional commander identified; all therefore omitted)

## NORTH-WEST FRONT (ARMY GROUP)

| | |
|---|---|
| General Officer Commanding | General of Cavalry Yakov Grigorevich Zhilinski (until 16 September) |
| Chief of Staff | Lieutenant General Oranovski |

## FIRST ARMY

| | |
|---|---|
| General Officer Commanding | General of Cavalry Pavel (Paul) Karlovich von Rennenkampf |
| Chief of Staff | Lieutenant General Mileant (until 11 September) |

### Infantry formations

| | |
|---|---|
| II Corps* 26th and 43rd divisions | General of Cavalry Scheidemann (until 31 August) |

* formally transferred from the Second Army, 22 August

III  Corps                          General of Infantry Yepanchin

25th and 27th divisions

IV  Corps                           General of Artillery Uliev

30th and 40th divisions

XX  Corps                           General of Infantry Smirnov

28th and 29th divisions

XXVI Corps †                        General of Infantry Gerncross

53rd and 56th reserve divisions

† into the line c. 31 August

54th, 72nd and 76th reserve divisions came into the line for the Battle of the Masurian Lakes;
57th, 68th and 73rd not used

## Rifle formation

5th Rifle Brigade

## Cavalry formations

1st Guard Cavalry Division     Lieutenant General Kasnakov

2nd Guard Cavalry Division     Lieutenant General Raukh

1st Cavalry Division           Lieutenant General Gurko

                               (7 September to Tenth Army)

2nd Cavalry Division           Lieutenant General Nahichevanski

3rd Cavalry Division           Lieutenant General Belgard

Between two and four of these divisions were at times formed into a Cavalry Corps under
Nahichevanski

1st Independent Cavalry        Major Genereal Oranovski

Brigade

## SECOND ARMY

| | |
|---|---|
| General Officer Commanding | General of Cavalry Alexander Vasilievich Samsonov (from 31 August, General of Cavalry Scheidemann) |
| Chief of Staff | Major General Postovski |

### Infantry formations

| | |
|---|---|
| I Corps* 22nd and 24th divisions | General of Infantry Artamonov (from 28 August, Lieutenant General Dushkevich) |
| VI Corps 4th and 16th divisions | General of Infantry Blagoveshchenski (until 12 September) |
| XIII Corps 1st and 36th divisions | Lieutenant General Klyuev |
| XV Corps 6th and 8th divisions | General of Infantry Martos |
| XXIII Corps | General of Infantry Kondratovich (from 29 August Lieutenant General Sirelius) |
| 2nd Division and 3rd Guard Division | |
| Guard Corps* 1st and 2nd Guard divisions | General of Cavalry Besovrasov |

*transferred from the First Army via North-West Front, 19 and 20 August respectively; the Guard Corps did not enter East Prussia

### Rifle formation

1st Rifle Brigade

### Cavalry formations

| | |
|---|---|
| 4th Cavalry Division | Lieutenant General Tolpygo |
| 6th Cavalry Division | Lieutenant General Roop |
| 15th Cavalry Division | Lieutenant General Lyubomirov |

## TENTH ARMY (not fully deployed)

| | |
|---|---|
| General Officer Commanding (designate) | General of Infantry Flug |
| Chief of Staff (designate) | Lieutenant General Markow |

### Infantry formations

| | |
|---|---|
| I Turkestan: two and a half battalions | General of Infantry Zherofezhov |
| III Siberian: four battalions | General of Infantry Radkevich* |
| XXII Finnish: three battalions | Lieutenant General Baron von den Brinken |

* took command of the partial army, after Rennenkampf had briefly controlled it

### Rifle formation

4th Finnish Rifle Regiment (partial)

### Cavalry formations

Two half-squadrons attached to I and XXII corps respectively

1st Cavalry Division detached from First Army on 7 September

# APPENDIX B:
## ORGANIZATION AND WEAPONRY

### RUSSIAN FORCES

On paper, every infantry division of 14,800 men comprised four regiments (each with four battalions and an eight-gun machine gun section), a cavalry squadron and a field artillery brigade of six batteries (each of eight guns, mainly 75–80mm with a few older 90mm models). Reinforcements for a division would comprise a second- or third-line Cossack cavalry regiment and two batteries of 120mm guns. The Russian corps had two infantry divisions, a division of light howitzers (two six-gun batteries, including the 1910 French model made under licence) and a battalion of engineers, consisting of a telegraph company and three engineer companies. One rifle brigade had four regiments (each of two battalions) and three field batteries (each eight guns). A cavalry brigade consisted of two regiments (each with six squadrons and a total strength of 1,040 sabres); a cavalry division comprised two brigades, a horse artillery division of two six-gun field batteries and a section of eight machine guns. Every cavalry corps had two to five cavalry divisions.

The infantry and cavalry were equipped with the Mosin-Nagant 1891 pattern rifle weighing 9.5 pounds; the militia (never committed to the front line) used the 1878 Berdanki rifle. The Maxim machine gun was in general use. The field and horse artillery attached to divisions used 1900 and 1902 model 3-inch quick-firing (QF) guns. Each corps had two six-gun batteries of 4.8-inch QF howitzers; every heavy artillery division two four-gun batteries of 6-inch howitzers (1910 model) and one four-gun battery of 4.2-inch guns.

Only seven of these divisions existed in peacetime, with a planned expansion to sixty-three on mobilization. Overall the Russians were credited with 244 aeroplanes and fifteen airships of dubious quality.

## GERMAN FORCES

The Germans were organized differently. Their infantry brigades comprised two regiments, each of three battalions (four companies) and a company of six machine guns. Each division consisted of two infantry brigades; a cavalry regiment; a field artillery brigade of two regiments (each with six batteries of six 75–105mm guns); a company of field engineers; bridging and telephone detachments. Reinforcements comprised a rifle brigade and four batteries of 150mm guns. A German infantry division totalled 17,500 men (12,000 rifles); 4,000 horses (600 sabres); twenty-four machine guns; seventy-two artillery pieces. Reserve divisions, though, had only thirty-six field guns. Every corps consisted of two divisions; its own attached engineering, bridging, telegraph and telephone detachments; a heavy artillery battalion of four batteries (four guns, 15cm howitzers or 21cm mortars); a *jäger* (light infantry) battalion. The full establishment comprised 44,000 men (25,000 rifles with a range of about 2,000 yards, similar to the Russian rifle); 15,000 horses (1,200 sabres); fifty-four machine guns; 160 guns. Reserve corps had only eighty-eight field pieces, no heavy guns and no attached aeroplanes. Each cavalry division had three brigades (two regiments of four squadrons); a horse artillery detachment (three batteries of four guns); three *jäger* battalions (each with a company of six machine guns); a separate battery of six machine guns; engineer, wireless, intelligence and motor transport detachments. However, in 1914 not every cavalry division possessed three *jäger* battalions. The full establishment of a cavalry division numbered 7,000 men (5,000 sabres); 5,500 horses; twenty-four machine guns; twelve field guns. Each Landwehr brigade comprised two regiments of three battalions; one cavalry squadron; one field battery. A squadron of six aeroplanes was allocated to each infantry corps and twelve aeroplanes to each army; a field detachment of two balloons was allotted to each army. The German Army, as a whole, deployed fifteen airships and an estimated 1,300 aeroplanes; all reputedly of better quality than their Russian counterparts. Königsberg and Allenstein, respectively situated in front of the Russian First and Second armies in East Prussia, and Thorn close by in West Prussia were airship depots.

# BIBLIOGRAPHY

The material below has been used during the preparation of this book. I am also extremely grateful for the assistance given to me for Russian language sources by Mike Pushkin (Head of Russian, Birmingham University), Michael Orr (Conflict Studies Research Centre, The Royal Military Academy Sandhurst) and my son Mark Sweetman (RIA Novosti, Moscow). Andrew Orgill and the staff of the Central Library, The Royal Military Academy Sandhurst, have as ever been enormously helpful with advice about available material and by securing the more obscure volumes for consultation. Works in Russian and Polish have not been listed, but specialists will find a wide range in the British Library.

## ENGLISH

Anon., *War Facts and Figures* (London: The British Dominions General Insurance Co. Ltd., 1915)

R.B. Asprey, *The First Battle of the Marne* (London: Weidenfeld & Nicolson, 1962)

R.B. Asprey, *The German High Command at War: Hindenburg & Ludendorff in the First World War* (London: Little, Brown, 1993)

J.W. Bennett, *Hindenburg, The Wooden Titan* (Hamden, Conn.: Archon Books, 1963)

O. von Bismarck, *Reflections and Reminiscences* (Eng. trs., London: Smith, Elder & Co.,1898), vol. 2.

Gen. A.A. Brussilov, *A Soldier's Note-Book 1914–1918* (Eng. trs., London: Macmillan & Son Ltd., 1930)

J. Buchan, *A History of the Great War* (London, Edinburgh and New York: Thomas Nelson & Sons Ltd, 1921), vol. 1.

C.R.M.F. Cruttwell, *A History of the Great War 1914–1918* (Oxford: Clarendon Press, 1936)

N. Davies, *A History of Poland: the Origins to 1795* (Oxford: Clarendon Press, 1981)

T.N. Dupuy, *1914: The Battles in the East* (New York: Franklin Watts Inc., 1967)

Brig. Gen. Sir J.E. Edmonds, *Military Operations France and Belgium 1914, August – October 1914* (London: Macmillan & Co., 1933)

G. Evans, *Tannenberg 1410/1914* (London: Hamish Hamilton, 1970)

M. Goldsmith and F. Voigt, *Hindenburg: the Man and the Legend* (London: Faber & Faber, 1930)

Lt. Gen. N.N. Golovine, *The Russian Army in the World War* (Eng. trs., New Haven: Yale University Press, 1931)

Lt. Gen. N.N. Golovine, *The Russian Campaign of 1914* (Eng. trs., London: Hugh Rees Ltd., 1933)

Gen. B Gourko.(Lt. Gen. V.I. Gurko), *Memories and Impressions of War and Revolution in Russia 1914–1917* (Eng. trs., London: John Murray, 1918)

O. Halecki, *The History of Poland* (London: J.M. Dent, 1942)

Marshal von Hindenburg, *Out of My Life* (Eng. trs., London: Cassell & Co., 1920)

Gen. M. von Hoffmann, *The War of Lost Opportunities* (Eng. trs., London: Kegan, Paul, Trench, Trubner & Co., 1924)

Maj. Gen. Sir Edmund Ironside, *Tannenberg: The First Thirty Days in East Prussia* (Edinburgh and London: William Blackwood & Sons Ltd., 1933)

Alexander von Kluck, *The March on Paris and the Battle of the Marne 1914* (Eng. trs., London: Edward Arnold, 1920)

Maj. Gen. Sir Arthur Knox, *With the Russian Army 1914–1917* (London: Hutchinson & Co., 1921)

B.H. Liddell Hart, *A History of the World War* (London: Faber & Faber, 1930)

V.S. Littauer, *Russian Hussar* (London: J.A. Allen & Co., 1965)

Gen. Ludendorff, *My War Memories 1914–1918* (Eng. trs., London: Hutchinson & Co., n.d.), vol. 1.

K. Macksey, 'Tannenberg', *History of the First World War* (Bristol: Purnell & Sons Ltd., 1969), vol. 1, no. 9.

B.W. Menning, *Bayonets Before Bullets, The Imperial Russian Army 1861–1914* (Bloomington and Indianapolis: Indiana University Press, 1992)

Lord Mottistone, *Fear, and Be Slain* (London: Hodder & Stoughton, 1937)

B. Moynahan, *The Claws of the Bear* (London and Sydney: Hutchinson, 1989)

Lt. Col. P. Neame, *German Strategy in the Great War* (London: Edward Arnold, 1923)

K.F. Novak, (ed.), *War Diaries and Other Papers of Major General Max Hoffmann* (Eng. trs., London: Martin Secker, 1929), 2 vols.

B. Pitt, 'Causes of the War', *History of the First World War* (Bristol: Purnell & Sons Ltd, 1969), vol. 1, no. 1.

C.W. Previté-Orton and Z.N. Brooke, *The Cambridge Medieval History* (Cambridge: Cambridge University Press, 1964), vols. 7 and 8.

W.H. Reddaway, J.H. Penson, O. Halecki, R. Dyboski (eds.), *The Cambridge History of Poland* (Cambridge: Cambridge University Press, 1950)

G. Ritter, *The Schlieffen Plan: Critique of a Myth* (Eng. trs., London: Oswald Wolf, 1958)

W. Rutherford, *The Russian Army in World War I* (London: Gordon Cremonesi, 1975)

D.E. Showalter, *Tannenberg, clash of empires* (Hamden, Conn.: Archon Books, 1991)

N. Stone, *The Eastern Front* (London: Hodder & Stoughton, 1975)

Military Correspondent of The Times, *The War in the Far East 1904-1905* (London: John Murray, 1905)

B.W. Tuchman, *August 1914* (London: Constable, 1962)

## GERMAN

S. Ekdahl, *Die Schlacht bei Tannenberg 1410* (Berlin: Duncker & Humbolt, 1982)

Gen. H. von Francois, *Marneschlacht und Tannenberg* (Berlin: August Schlerl, n.d.)

Gen. C.A.M. Hoffmann, *Tannenberg, wie es wirklich war* (Berlin: Verlag für Kulturpolitik, 1926)

Gen. Helmuth von Moltke, *Erinnerungen* (Stuttgart: Der Kommende Tag Verlag, 1922)

Gen. von Morgen, *Meiner Truppen Heldenkampfe* (Berlin: E. Mittler & Sohn, 1920)

Reichsarchiv, *Der Weltkrieg 1914 bis 1918 'Die Grenzschlachten im Westen'* (Berlin: E. Mittler & Sohn, 1925), Band 1.

Reichsarchiv, *Die Weltkrieg 1914 bis 1918 'Die Befreiung Ostpreussens'* (Berlin: E. Mittler & Sohn, 1925), Band 2.

W. von Stephani, *Mit Hindenburg bei Tannenberg* (Berlin: R. Eisenschmidt, 1919)

W.A. Suhomlinov, *Erinnerungen* (Berlin: Verlag Hobbing, 1924)

Gen. von Tappen, *Bis zur Marne 1914* (Berlin: Verlag Gerhard Stalling, 1920)

# NOTES

## PREFACE

1. B.H. Liddell Hart, *A History of the World War 1914-1918* (London: Faber & Faber, 1930), p. 109.

## PROLOGUE: HISTORICAL LEGACY

1. C.W. Previté-Orton and Z.N. Brooke, *The Cambridge Medieval History* (Cambridge: Cambridge University Press, vol.8, p. 571; Jungingen quoted G. Evans, *Tannenberg 1410/1914* (London: Hamish Hamilton, 1970), p. 34.
2. Heralds and Jagiello quoted Evans, *Tannenberg*, p. 40.
3. Polish squadron quoted Evans, *Tannenberg*, p. 42.
4. W.H. Reddaway, J.H. Penson, O. Halecki and R. Dyboski (eds.), *The Cambridge History of Poland* (Cambridge: Cambridge University Press, 1950), p. 214.
5. Marshal von Hindenburg, *Out of My Life* (Eng. trs, London: Cassell & Co., 1920), p. 3.

## CHAPTER 1: EDGE OF AN ABYSS

1. O. von Bismarck, *Reflections and Reminiscences* (Eng. trs, London: Smith, Elder & Co., 1898), vol. 2, pp. 283 and 282.
2. August 1912 agreement quoted in B.W. Menning, *Bayonets Before Bullets* (Indiana University Press, Bloomington and Indianapolis, 1992), p. 245; August 1913 agreement quoted in N. Stone, *The Eastern Front* (London: Hodder & Stoughton, 1975), p. 308, chap. 3 n. 2; Lt. Gen. N.N. Golovine, *The Russian Campaign of 1914* (Eng. trs, London: Hugh Rees Ltd.,1933), p. 55.

3. G. Ritter, *The Schlieffen Plan: Critique of a Myth* (Eng. trs, London: Oswald Wolf, 1958), p. 18.

4. Gen. M. von Hoffmann, *The War of Lost Opportunities* (Eng. trs, London: Kegan, Paul, Trench, Trubner & Co., 1924), p. 2.

5. Ritter, *Schlieffen Plan*, pp. 5 and 6.

6. Ritter, *Schlieffen Plan*, p. 8.

7. German general quoted B. Pitt 'Causes of the War', *History of the First World War* (Bristol: Purnell & Sons Ltd., 1969), vol. 1, no. 1, p. 31.

8. Golovine, *1914 Campaign*, p. 37.

9. Golovine, *1914 Campaign*, p. 38.

10. Bismarck quoted B.W. Tuchman, *August 1914* (London: Constable, 1962), p. 78; Nicholas II and Bethmann-Hollweg quoted J. Buchan, *A History of the Great War* (London, Edinburgh and New York: Thomas Nelson K Son Ltd, 1921), vol. 1, pp. 60 and 77 respectively.

## CHAPTER 2: MANOEUVRING FOR COMBAT

1. Gen. A.A. Brussilov, *A Soldier's Note-Book 1914–1918* (Eng. trs, London: Macmillan & Son Ltd., 1930), p. 1.

2. Anon., *War Facts and Figures* (London: The British Dominions General Insurance Co. Ltd., 1915), p. 48; Brussilov, *Soldier's Note-Book*, p. 18.

3. Brussilov, *Soldier's Note-Book*, p. 14.

4. Golovine, *1914 Campaign,* p. 26.

5. Golovine, *1914 Campaign*, pp. 33–4; Sazonov quoted Tuchman, *August 1914*, p. 70.

6. Brussilov, *Soldier's Note-Book*, p. 11.

7. Stone, *Eastern Front*, p. 27.

8. Brussilov, *Soldier's Note-Book*, p. 34.

9. Brussilov, *Soldier's Note-Book*, p. 28.

10. Maj. Gen. Sir A. Knox, *With the Russian Army 1914–1917* (London: Hutchinson & Co., 1921), p. 46.

11. Military Correspondent of The Times, *The War in the Far East 1904–1905*

(London: John Murray, 1905), pp. 330 and 534.

12. Knox, *Russian Army*, pp. 59 and 60.

13. B. Gourko (Gurko), *Memories and Impressions of War and Revolution in Russia 1914–1917* (Eng. trs London: John Murray, 1918), p. 35.

14. Hoffmann, *Lost Opportunities*, pp. 12 and 13.

15. Hoffmann, *Lost Opportunities*, pp. 13 and 1; K.F. Novak (ed.), *War Diaries and Other Papers of Major General Max Hoffmann* (Eng. trs, London: Martin Secker, 1929), vol. i, p. 37.


## CHAPTER 3: ADVANCE TO CONTACT

1. Rodzianko quoted W. Rutherford, *The Russian Army in World War I* (London: Gordon Cremonesi, 1975), p. 8; Knox, *Russian Army*, p. 40.

2. Brussilov, *Soldier's Note-Book*, pp. 6 and 7.

3. Paléologue quoted Golovine, *1914 Campaign*, p. 88; Yanushkevich quoted Evans, p. 70.

4. Yanushkevich quoted Golovine, *1914 Campaign*, p. 92; Yanushkevich's instructions to Zhilinski, 10 August 1914, Maj. Gen. Sir E. Ironside, *Tannenberg: The First Thirty Days in East Prussia* (London and Edinburgh: William Blackwood & Sons Ltd., 1933), pp. 42–3; Zhilinski to Yanushkevich, 12 August 1914, Ironside, *First Thirty Days*, p. 44.

5. Instruction No. 1, 13 August 1914, Zhilinski to the First Army, Ironside, *First Thirty Days,* pp. 44–6 and Golovine, *1914 Campaign*, App. 6, pp. 396–7.

6. Instruction No. 2, 13 August 1914, Zhilinski to the Second Army, Ironside, *First Thirty Days*, pp. 46–8.

7. Knox, *Russian Army,* 41; Golovine, *1914 Campaign*, p. 86.

8. Hoffmann, *Lost Opportunities*, pp. 14 and 15.

9. German Eighth Army Orders, 14 August 1914, Golovine, *1914 Campaign*, App. 7, pp. 398–9; Hoffmann diary entry, 13 August 1914, Novak, *War Diaries*, p. 37.

10. V.S. Littauer, *Russian Hussar* (London: J.A. Allen & Co., 1965), pp. 132 and 133.

11. Littauer, *Russian Hussar*, pp. 133 and 134.

12. Littauer, *Russian Hussar*, pp. 134, 135 and 137.

13. Gurko, *Memories and Impressions*, p. 31.

14. Hoffmann, *Lost Opportunities*, pp. 17 and 18.

15. Francois quoted Golovine, *1914 Campaign*, 113; Hoffmann, *Lost Opportunities*, p. 18.

16. Nahichevanski and Rennenkampf quoted Golovine, *1914 Campaign*, pp. 116 and 117 respectively.

17. Golovine, *1914 Campaign*, p. 114.

18. Russian observer quoted K. Macksey 'Tannenberg', *Purnell History*, p. 236.

19. Post-operational report, 28th Division Chief of Staff, quoted Golovine, *1914 Campaign*, p. 128; Golovine, *1914 Campaign*, p. 127.

20. Hesse quoted Golovine, *1914 Campaign*, p. 133.

21. Hoffmann, *Lost Opportunities*, p. 19; Hesse quoted Golovine, *1914 Campaign,* p. 134.

22. Oranovski quoted Golovine, *1914 Campaign*, p. 125.

23. Hoffmann, *Lost Opportunities*, p. 20.

24. Prittwitz quoted Hoffmann, *Lost Opportunities*, p. 20.

25. 20 August 1914, Prittwitz to Moltke quoted Evans, *Tannenberg*, p. 94; Prittwitz quoted Stone, *Eastern Front*, p. 61; Hoffmann diary entry, 21 August; Novak, *War Diaries*, p. 39.

26. Hoffmann, *Lost Opportunities*, p. 22.

27. Hindenburg, *My Life*, pp. 69, 72 and 81.

28. Gen. E. Ludendorff, *My War Memories 1914–1918* (Eng. trs., London: Hutchinson & Co., n.d.), vol. 1, pp. 9 and 12–13; Hindenburg, *My Life*, p. 84.

29. Moltke and Stein letters quoted Ludendorff, *War Memories*, pp. 41 and 42 respectively.

30. Ludendorff, *War Memories*, p. 44.

31. Ludendorff, *War Memories*, p. 46.

32. Ludendorff, *War Memories*, p. 46; Hindenburg, *My Life*, p. 83.

33. Ludendorff, *War Memories*, pp. 15 and 47.

34. Hoffmann, *Lost Opportunities*, p. 24; Hindenburg, *My Life*, p. 91; Hoffmann diary entry, 23 August, Novak, *War Diaries*, p. 40.

35. Golovine, *1914 Campaign*, p. 159.

## CHAPTER 4: TANNENBERG

1. Klyuev quoted Golovine, *1914 Campaign*, p. 170.

2. Second Army Orders, 14 August 1914, and Second Army Directive No. 1, 16 August 1914, Golovine, *1914 Campaign*, App. 12, pp. 404–5 and App. 13, pp. 405–6 respectively.

3. 19 August 1914, Samsonov to Zhilinski, and eyewitness, Golovine, *1914 Campaign*, p. 183.

4. 22 August 1914, Zhilinski signal to Samsonov, Golovine, *1914 Campaign*, p. 185; staff officer and Klyuev quoted Evans, *Tannenberg*, p. 103.

5. Martos quoted Macksey, *Purnell History*, p. 238; Gurko, *Memories and Impressions*, p. 29; Knox, *Russian Army*, p. 57.

6. Samsonov quoted Golovine, *1914 Campaign*, p. 188.

7. Knox, *Russian Army*, p. 64.

8. Zhilinski quoted Ironside, *First Thirty Days*, p. 134.

9. Second Army Directive No. 4, 23 August 1914, Golovine, *1914 Campaign*, App. 15, pp. 407–8.

10. Postovski quoted Knox, *Russian Army*, p. 61.

11. Knox, *Russian Army*, pp. 63, 66 and 67.

12. North-West Front HQ to Second Army and Zhilinski to Filimonov quoted Golovine, *1914 Campaign*, p. 204.

13. Hindenburg, *My Life*, p. 88.

14. Hindenburg, *My Life,* p. 92.

15. Hoffmann, *Lost Opportunities*, p. 28; Ludendorff, *Memories*, p. 9.

16. Ludendorff, *War Memories*, pp. 48, 50 and 49.

17. Hindenburg, *My Life,* p. 93.

18. Hindenburg, *My Life,* p. 94.

19. Ludendorff, *War Memories*, p. 50; Hindenburg, *My Life*, p. 95.

20. Knox, *Russian Army*, p. 67.

21. Servinovich quoted Ironside, *First Thirty Days*, p. 155.

22. Zhilinski and Rennenkampf quoted Ironside, *First Thirty Days*, pp. 200 and 202 respectively.

23. Ludendorff, *War Memories*, p. 51; Hindenburg, *My Life*, p. 95.

24. Knox, *Russian Army*, p. 69.

25. Knox, *Russian Army*, p. 71.

26. Knox, *Russian Army*, pp. 70 and 72.

27. Samsonov quoted Evans, *Tannenberg*, p. 132.

28. Ludendorff quoted Ironside, *First Thirty Days*, p. 177.

29. Hindenburg, *My Life*, p. 96; Samsonov quoted Ironside, *First Thirty Days*, p. 182.

30. Knox, *Russian Army*, p. 73.

31. Knox, *Russian Army*, p. 73 and  Samsonov quoted p. 74.

32. Martos quoted Macksey, *Purnell History*, p. 240.

33. Ludendorff's orders timed 9.40 and 12.25 quoted Ironside, *First Thirty Days*, pp. 271 and 272.

34. Ludendorff, *War Memories*, p. 55.

35. Samsonov quoted Ironside, *First Thirty Days*, p. 291.

36. Knox, *Russian Army*, p. 76.

37. Ludendorff, *War Memories*, p. 57; Hindenburg, *My Life*, p. 96.

38. Eighth Army Orders, 29 August 1914, Golovine, *1914 Campaign*, App. 17, pp. 409–10.

39. Gurko, *Memories and Impressions*, p. 51.

40. Staff officer quoted Golovine, *1914 Campaign*, p. 319; Ludendorff, *War Memories*, p. 57; Russian survivor quoted Macksey, *Purnell History*, p. 241.

41. Heeder quoted Evans, *Tannenberg*, p. 155; Ludendorff, *War Memories*, p. 57.

42. Hindenburg, *My Life*, p. 98.

43. Gurko, *Memories and Impressions*, pp. 53 and 54; Littauer, *Russian Hussar*, p. 160.

44. Gurko, *Memories and Impressions*, pp. 54 and 55; Littauer, *Russian Hussar*, p. 163.

45. Samsonov quoted Ironside, *First Thirty Days*, p. 188.

46. Hindenburg, *My Life*, p. 98.

47. Hindenburg, *My Life*, p. 99.

48. Ludendorff, *War Memories*, pp. 57–8; Hindenburg, *My Life*, p. 99; Hoffmann, *Lost Opportunities*, p. 24

49. Gurko, *Memories and Impressions*, pp. 59 and 60.

50. Ludendorff, *War Memories*, pp. 58 and 57; Hoffmann diary entry, 30 August, Novak, *War Diaries*, p. 40.

51. Heeder quoted Evans, *Tannenberg*, p. 156; Hoffmann diary entry, 30 August 1914, Novak, *War Diaries*, p. 40.


## CHAPTER 5: MASURIAN LAKES

1. North-West Front HQ quoted Ironside, *First Thirty Days*, p. 193.

2. GHQ directive to North-West Front, 31 August 1914, quoted Golovine, *1914 Campaign*, p. 332.

3. GHQ to Postovski quoted Ironside, *First Thirty Days*, p. 193.

4. Oranovski and Mileant quoted Golovine, *1914 Campaign,*pp. 339 and 340 respectively.

5. Russian staff officer quoted Golovine, *1914 Campaign*, p. 341.

6. Ludendorff, *War Memories*, p. 60.

7. Ironside, *First Thirty Days*, p. 206.

8. Zhilinski quoted Ironside, *First Thirty Days*, p. 211; Hindenburg, *My Life*, p. 102.

9. Zhilinski quoted Golovine, *1914 Campaign*, p. 343.

10. Zhilinski to Rennenkampf telegram, 4 September 1914, Golovine, *1914 Campaign,* pp. 343–4; North-West Front directive, 5 September 1914, Golovine, *1914 Campaign*, p. 344.

11. Hindenburg, *My Life*, p. 99; Ludendorff, *War Memories*, p. 62.

12. Hindenburg, *My Life*, pp. 101 and 103.

13. Ludendorff, *War Memories*, p. 62; Hindenburg, *My Life*, p. 101.

14. Hoffmann, *Lost Opportunities*, p. 36.

15. Hindenburg, *My Life*, pp. 105 and 104.

16. Zhilinski quoted Golovine, *1914 Campaign*, p. 356.

17. Ludendorff, *War Memories*, p. 62.

18. Hindenburg, *My Life*, p. 105.

19. Ludendorff, *War Memories*, p. 111.

20. Hindenburg, *My Life,* p. 110; Hoffmann, *Lost Opportunities*, p. 38.

21. Ludendorff, *War Memories*, p. 65; Hoffmann, *Lost Opportunities*, p. 39.

22. Hindenburg, *My Life*, p. 107; Ludendorff, *War Memories*, p. 66

23. Hindenburg, *My Life*, pp. 108 and 107.

24. Littauer, *Russian Hussar*, p. 170.

25. Zhilinski quoted Ironside, *First Thirty Days*, p. 244; Yanushkevich and Grand Duke Nikolai quoted Macksey, *Purnell History*, p. 245.

26. Hoffmann diary entry, 15 September 1914, Novak, *War Diaries*, p. 42.

## EPILOGUE: COUNTING THE COST

1. Hoffmann, *Lost Opportunities*, p. 34.

2. Knox, *Russian Army*, p. 85; Hindenburg, *My Life*, p. 102.

3. Stone, *Eastern Front*, p. 63; Golovine, *1914 Campaign*, p. 195.

4. Golovine, *1914 Campaign*, p. 325.

5. Golovine, *1914 Campaign*, pp. 59, 390 and 73; Bismarck quoted Buchan, *Great War*, p. 73.

6. Tappen quoted Evans, p. 162; Foch preface to Golovine, *1914 Campaign*, pp. ix–x; Ludendorff, *War Memories*, p. 69.

7. Lord Mottistone, *Fear, and be Slain* (London: Hodder & Stoughton, 1937), p. 221.

8. Liddell Hart, *World War*, p. 115.

9. Hoffmann, *Lost Opportunities*, p. 90; 1925 letter, Francois to Hoffmann quoted Novak, *War Diaries*, p. 19; Hoffmann on Ludendorff, diary entry, 4 September 1914, Novak, *War Diaries*, p. 41.

10. Knox, *Russian Army*, p. 86; Heintzelman foreword to Golovine, *1914 Campaign*, p. vii.

# INDEX

# PICTURE CREDITS